WHEN BROTHERS DWELL TOGETHER

Seminarians of the Pontifical College Josephinum

As Told To:

J. F. Leahy

The Josephinum Press
Columbus, Ohio

COVER PHOTOGRAPH:

The Josephinum in Springtime

(credit C. DiNovo, PCJ. Used with permission)

ISBN-13: 978-0692211168

ISBN-10: 0692211160

Library of Congress Control Number: 2014908635
JOSEPHINUM PRESS, COLUMBUS, OHIO

How good and how pleasant it is,
When brothers dwell together as one!
Like fine oil on the head
Running down upon the beard.
Upon the beard of Aaron,
Upon the collar of his robe.
Psalm 133

For my grandsons:
Jackson, Joseph and Anthony James
"My sons have sons, as brave as were their fathers"
(Caitlín Ní Uallacháin, W.B. Yeats, 1902)

TABLE OF CONTENTS

*GALLERIES OF PHOTOGRAPHS MAY BE FOUND FOLLOW-
ING CHAPTER THREE AND CHAPTER SIX.*

Reverend Monsignor Christopher J. Schreck, PHD, STD, Sixteenth Rector/President of the Pontifical College Josephinum since 2012.

[Photo credit: Carolyn Dinovo – PCJ]

FOREWORD

The name *Joseph* reverberates throughout Judeo-Christian Salvation History. Both the Old Testament Joseph, the son of Jacob/Israel, and the New Testament Joseph, the husband of Mary and guardian of the Christ-child, were known for their dreams. Both the Book of Genesis and the Gospel according to Matthew describe how God communicated so effectively with each of them, and prophetically pointed them to their future vocation and mission by means of dreams. Genesis Chapter 37 begins the story of Joseph, reports two of his dreams (Genesis 37:5-8; Genesis 37:9-11), and has his brothers describe him as that "master dreamer" (Genesis 37:19). Matthew 1:16 begins the story of Joseph, reports that he was the son of another Jacob and the betrothed of Mary, with the stipulation that it was "of her [emphasis added] was born Jesus who was called the Messiah." In the New Testament, Joseph is instructed in dreams to "take Mary, your wife into your home" (Matthew 1:20), as well as to "rise, take the child and his mother and flee to Egypt and stay there until I tell you" (Matthew 2:13); and again, "rise, take the child and his mother and go to the land of Israel" (Matthew 2:20). In each case, Joseph followed his dream, fulfilled the Lord's instructions, and accomplished his mission.

Monsignor Joseph Jessing, following a vocation to the priesthood, left his native Germany to pursue another kind of dream – to serve

German immigrants in the United States as a Catholic priest. Msgr. Jessing's story of vision and courage was animated by his desire to care for the German and German-speaking Catholics who had been transplanted to America and who had found a new life here in Ohio. Jessing was especially motivated to care for children who had been orphaned; when a number of young men in his orphanage began to express their wish to follow their own dreams to the priesthood, Msgr. Jessing took the far-reaching step of establishing a seminary dedicated to St. Joseph, his patron, in 1888 in Columbus, Ohio, thus fulfilling his dream to provide for the future of the Church in the United States into the 20th and now 21st centuries. For more than 125 years, spanning three different centuries, and now two different millennia, the Pontifical College Josephinum has fulfilled its mission of priestly formation and continued the farsighted dream of Msgr. Joseph Jessing.

Only four years after its founding, the Josephinum was granted pontifical status in 1892 by Pope Leo XIII and remains to this day the only pontifical seminary outside of Italy, a circumstance that indicates its special character and the scope of its mission. The institution is devotedly at the service of the Holy See; fidelity to the mission of the Holy Father and attentiveness to his directives are especially important aspects of the life of the seminary. The Josephinum expresses that attentiveness in its effort to orient all its programs toward the preparation of men to serve the New Evangelization which Pope Saint John Paul II, and subsequent pontiffs, declared to be vital to the mission of the Church at the beginning of the third millennium.

In keeping with its broad mission, the Josephinum has educated priestly candidates for many dioceses in the United States and abroad, as well as for religious orders and secular institutes. The Josephinum seeks to prepare men to serve the Lord faithfully as priests wherever they are called and sent to do so. Nonetheless, the Josephinum emphasizes the preparation of priests for service in the United States of America. As part of its mission to serve the Church in the United States, the Josephinum prepares seminarians for priestly ministry to Catholics in this country, as well as seminarians who may hail originally from other parts of the world for priestly ministry either in the United States or in their native countries. The Josephinum thereby offers an education that is appropriate for priestly ministry in the universal Church and that is deeply rooted in the Catholic Tradition, in a way that is apt for a global and diverse society.

More than a century and a quarter later, Monsignor Joseph Jessing's dream of educating men to serve the People of God continues to be realized. In almost all of the past seven years, the Josephinum has experienced a marked increase in enrollment, in keeping with the national phenomenon of a renaissance in religious vocations in the United States. The Josephinum began the 2013-14 year of formation with the highest enrollment of collegians, pre-theologians and theologians it has seen in 49 years.

On a recent visit to the Josephinum, Archbishop Carlo Maria Viganò, Apostolic Nuncio to the United States and Chancellor of the Josephinum, spoke to the increase in enrollment and in diocesan representation at the Josephinum, where the seminarians' ethnic and cultural backgrounds mirror the diversity of the Church in the United States as whole. "The very fact that the Josephinum is becoming more and more universal in the composition of its members is bringing the richness of different cultures and opening new horizons for evangelization of the Church in America," Archbishop Viganò said. He also said the Vatican feels "a great consideration for this institution" given its status as a pontifical seminary, and heralded the Josephinum as "a sign of great hope for the Catholic Church in this country."

The Josephinum is, indeed, a sign of great hope, and it is the entire seminary community that makes it so. Faculty and staff of the highest caliber and dedication diligently work to the best of their ability to further the mission of the seminary.

Mr. Jack Leahy joined the staff of the Josephinum in 2006, after a lengthy and successful career in the defense intelligence community and telecommunication industry. His tireless efforts and unrelenting energy enabled and prepared the seminary to embark on a new venture – a distance learning program for permanent deacons in the United States. Since its inception, the program has grown to serve deacons from dioceses across the country, and now provides a critical avenue by which these men may fulfill the continuing education requirements set forth in the National Directory for the Formation, Ministry and Life of Permanent Deacons in the United States, published by the United States Conference of Catholic Bishops in 2005.

Mr. Leahy dedicated a number of years to the Josephinum, working closely with the administration to ensure the development and integrity of distance learning programs. He retired officially in 2011, but has remained an active and engaged member of the seminary community, stemming from a sincere investment in and affection for this historic institution and its seminarians.

Mr. Leahy has crafted this book to capture the stories and the dreams of many of our current seminarians, who relate in their own words the joys and challenges of priestly discernment and preparation. These are men who love the Church, are fervent in their desire to preach the Gospel, and are dedicated defenders of all that is good and true in the world around them. The friendships that are forged among those who study at the Josephinum grow and deepen with each passing year, witnessed by the many expressions of friendship, prayer, and encouragement that take place among them. While life in community is not without its challenges, we are given in abundance the gifts of charity and fraternity that help us to remain dedicated to and focused on our mission.

Truly, it is an honor for me and for all the members of our faculty and staff to serve this extraordinary institution and the seminarians who live, work, and study here. It is an honor to support them on their path of discernment and preparation and to be inspired by their stories of vocation and mission. Each of us – faculty, staff, and seminarians of the past, present, and future – shares the privilege of being members of the Josephinum family, custodians of Monsignor Jessing's dream, and adopted children of Saint Joseph, Monsignor Jessing's patron and our own.

Rev. Monsignor Christopher J. Schreck, PHD, STD
Sixteenth Rector/President of the Pontifical College Josephinum
May 1, 2014 —The Feast of St. Joseph the Worker

1 DISCERNING YOUR VOCATION

"The first thing that started my discernment process was receiving a pamphlet in the mail from a religious organization which asked if I had ever considered becoming a priest. I was 24 years old and struggling with what I wanted to do with my life...when I received that pamphlet, I took it as a sign that God was answering my question...When I finally felt ready to enter the seminary, I did it with joy and excitement, and have never looked back." **Edward Shikina— Fourth Year Pre-Theology—Columbus, OH—[Diocese of Columbus]**

"I had an interest in the priesthood from a young age and began to investigate the call more throughout high school. I attended a live-in during the fall of 2002, my senior year in high school. I went to a university instead of applying to seminary and the call remained in the back and sometimes front of my mind throughout college and after graduation. I continued to speak with a trusted priest friend through these years, which was very helpful in my discernment and kept me thinking about the priesthood. I finally began the application process in December 2008 and entered in fall 2009." **Michael Hartge—Third Year Theology—Reynoldsburg, OH—]Diocese of Columbus]**

Discerning one's vocation is not just about making good choices such as what to eat today, what to name your new dog, or who to ask to the prom. On the contrary, discernment is all about developing a relationship with God so that we can see our life as God sees it, and accept the plan that the Creator has in store for us.

Discernment helps us become more aware of what is going on in our daily life, to be more sensitive to our deeper desires and hopes, as well as our reactions or responses to the world around us.

Each of us is different: Our unique gifts and personalities, our life experiences and family backgrounds shape our world view and what we have to offer. Consider the very different experiences of several other seminarians at the Pontifical College Josephinum:

"I am from Mindat Town, Southern Chin State, Myanmar. I have two siblings, a brother and a sister. I am the oldest in my family. My Dad was a policeman. He has passed away. My Mom makes traditional wine for our living and my younger brother is working in Malaysia now. We have a very different culture. Family bonding is so great. We live for one another. So, answering the call of God is a great challenge too.

I witnessed the incredible examples of my parish priest, Msgr. Polinus and way he cares for the needy and the poor both in a spiritual and physical sense. I would say he is one of my role models; since my childhood I understood that the joy of giving self for other was so great, free, whole etc. My mom wanted me to study in my own country so that I could visit her a least once a year. My younger brother thought as a young man I should choose a greater challenge. Both of them supported my decision.

I consulted with my bishop, my parish priest and some of my priest friends. My bishop who had been in the United States told me that it would be hard for me, but prayer and perseverance would reward me.

When I heard the news that I was coming to this seminary I was really excited. I looked up the pictures of the Josephinum before coming here and I did not know what to think about it in my mind. My first impression during my earliest weeks here was that everybody knew my name and called me by my name even though I did not know them. They were very friendly to me, and asked me if I needed any help. I noticed that they liked to pray a lot!" **Ling Khui Shing (Anthony) – First Year Theology- Mindat Town, Southern Chin State, [Diocese of Taunggyi, Myanmar]**

"I am the middle child between two twin older brothers who are 34, a younger sister, a younger brother, and a recently adopted 2 year old brother who is the child of one of my older brothers. I have three grandparents from Mexico and one from Pittsburgh, P.A. This is where the name "Wetzel" comes from. I come from a huge Mexican family with over 40 first cousins and a multitude of cousins and relatives.

I believe the example of holy priests in my life greatly influenced me, especially my own bishop, Bishop Thomas J. Olmsted. They seemed to live a life that was real and had an authenticity about them that I did not. I have come to learn that these holy men in my life were grounded in their identity as a beloved son of the Father and gave a witness to true fatherhood.

Discovering my vocation was a slow gradual process. I began to have a stirring for priesthood when I started to altar serve in sixth grade. This developed slowly as I went into high school. It was not until sophomore year, however, that I really became engaged in my faith and comfortable with priesthood. During that year I learned that I was not just a face in the crowd, but God knew me by name and had a plan for me. He wanted me to be a saint! From there I continued going to youth group and talking to different priests.

Although I began to really consider priesthood in my sophomore year of high school, I wasn't committed to seminary until December of my Senior Year. Seminary seemed like a big step for me and I had some fear about it since I had never visited the Josephinum. I entered a discernment retreat asking the Lord to show me what he wanted to show me, because I didn't know where I was going after seminary. During the retreat, while the application process was being explained, I received a cringing feeling that I should apply to seminary. It kind of spooked me a bit. After the retreat I went home immediately and prayed about it. As I was kneeling at my bed, I felt a great peace, joy, and excitement at the prospect of going to seminary. I immediately emailed the Vocations Director and set up a meeting.

I consulted a great deal with my pastor, school chaplain and vocations director. One key piece of advice that they gave was to stick close to the Lord. Go to adoration, attend confession more regularly, assist at daily Mass when possible. For it is when we are close to the Lord, he is able to speak to us.

In our diocese, the application process starts with something like a 38 page application. This includes personal information, short answers, and a 6-8 page autobiography. You are also in need of letters of recommendation and physicals. After the application is submitted, the Vocations Director sends you to a psychologist to receive a psych evaluation. This takes about 4-5 hours with a break in between. After the psych evaluation is finished, the candidate is placed before a review board composed of a priest, sister, deacon and a male and female lay person. They ask you various questions about your life and the application. At the conclusion of the interview, they compile a report which is then forwarded to the bishop, along with the psych evaluation and application for his decision.

My family had kind of grown accustomed to the possibility of me being a priest by this time. My mom used to say she wanted grand-children, but by senior year, they were very happy with my decision. It was very much a joy to share with them the news and they were very supportive.

I really had not a clue about the Josephinum before I came here. I even showed up late to orientation because I was at World Youth Day. So it was a whirlwind to go straight from Europe to seminary. I remember seeing the tower for the first time and being very excited that this would be my new home.

As soon as I arrived, holy hour was occurring in St. Turibius. I remember it being very hot and humid. I fell asleep in the cha-pel and woke up for Evening prayer! I was completely surprised when they started chanting the Psalms. I did not even know that they would do that. Besides that, my first weeks were good. I remember everyone being warm and welcoming. It was very easy to make friends, but I was very shy for the first couple weeks. I also had a beard at the time, and people thought I was middle east-ern." **Estevan Wetzel—Fourth Year College—Phoenix, AZ.— [Diocese of Phoenix]**

God does not call us to become someone we are not. Instead, God lovingly calls us to be the best version of ourselves, living our lives in the world in the same way that Jesus did.

Discerning our vocation, then, means discovering how God invites us to live out the gift of who we are in the world. Another way of looking at it is to ask: How might God be calling us to put ourselves, with all ours strengths and, yes, our many weaknesses, at the service of others?

The context of our discernment, and the foundation of our vocation, is our relationship with God. As as we begin the process, it is important to be living a full Christian life. Only then can we:

- Embrace our own life and the lives of others as beautiful gifts of the Creator.

- Take time to meditate on the gift of our lives and focusing on gratitude in prayer.

- Grow in our relationship with Jesus and his Church through prayer and the sacraments.

- Take time to pray every day, especially praying with the Word of God. Participate fully at Mass at least weekly, and seek to imitate Jesus more closely in our daily life, living in daily conversion and participating often in the Sacrament of Reconciliation.

- Live as disciples of Christ by growing in our knowledge and love of the Catholic faith, and our desire to share our faith through the new evangelization.

- Study our faith and seek to live it by serving in our parish or in another ministry that appeals to us.

When we are living a full Christian life, it is easier for us to recognize God's intention for our lives. There are many paths to the Lord!

"Both of my parents were born and raised in the Philippines. They came to America in 1991, right before I was born, because they did not want to raise their family in the political and social turmoil occurring in the Philippines. I have two younger siblings: Isabella (17) and Francis

(14). When I was about 10 years old, my father was diagnosed with a rare type of Parkinson's disease. My mother's example of sacrificial love has been a source of unending inspiration for me and my pursuit of God's will for my life.

My parents did the best that they could to raise me and two younger siblings in an environment of prayer and faith in God. We went to Mass every Sunday, attended weekly catechesis, and prayed before meals and bed time. The faith was something we did as a family, but it was not yet personal.

The summer before my junior year of high school, I went with my youth group to a Steubenville Youth Conference in Tucson, AZ. For the first time in my life, I encountered other people, even peers, who were passionate about the faith and desired to love and serve God. It was during Eucharistic Adoration at that conference that I experienced Christ's love for me for the first time and this love set my heart ablaze. Later, during the spring of my senior year, I attended a youth retreat for the Diocese of Phoenix. During Eucharistic adoration, I felt the love of Christ as if it pierced my heart like never before. I wasn't quite sure what was happening, but all I could do was cry uncontrollably. My youth minister approached me to console me. I told her, without knowing exactly what this meant, 'I feel as if God is calling me to die to myself'. She smiled and left me, instructing me to continue praying.

Immediately after Eucharistic Adoration, the men and women were divided. The women got to talk with a group of sisters and the men had a session with about five priests of the Diocese of Phoenix, as well as the Bishop of Phoenix, Most Reverend Thomas J. Olmsted.

I had never in my life thought about a vocation to the priesthood before, but as the priests and the bishop were speaking about their vocation stories and their lives as priests, I could feel my heart pounding and burning excitedly. I could tell that they were radiating pure love and joy and I deeply desired that. I thought to myself, 'What if I were called to be a priest?'

I had already been accepted to Franciscan University in Steubenville, Ohio to study Political Science and Economics. After the retreat described above, I learned about Franciscan's Priestly Discernment Program. Through God's providence I applied, was accepted, and they informed me about the scholarships they were able to give due to many generous benefactors. Because of this program, I was able to attend Franciscan University as I had so desired since my initial conversion at the youth conference.

I attended Franciscan University of Steubenville for four years, all the while pursuing a degree in philosophy and theology and receiving top-notch formation and guidance in discernment of a priestly vocation in the Priestly Discernment Program.

Each year got more challenging, but more and more beautiful. My senior year at Franciscan was particularly filled with challenges, even to the point of doubting a next step to the seminary.

Finally though, during Christmas break of my senior year in college, I finally chose to pursue the priesthood with all my heart trusting in the Lord's love, guidance, and providence. I began my application for the Diocese of Phoenix. It was a very long, but thorough application. I appreciated it because it showed me how much effort is put in to the Church's discernment of her own potential priests. The psychological tests were also very fruitful. I was accepted May 24th, 2013.

I didn't know much about the Josephinum. I graduated from Franciscan, got accepted as a seminarian, and then packed my bags for Columbus

8

*I was immediately drawn to the special charisms of the Josephinum; that
it began as an orphanage and that it is, as Monsignor Schreck said in
his rector's address last semester, pontifical, national, and missionary. I
knew immediately that I was part of something special.*

*I have recently begun my second semester of 1st Theology at the
Josephinum and am constantly falling deeper in love with the Lord
and His Church. The priests I have known have helped me understand myself better and the ways in which God has specially created
me. Specifically, though, I would say Bishop Olmsted. He is such an
example of a loving and wise Father who is entirely given over to God.
I first encountered him at a youth retreat my freshman year of HS and
in the eight years that I have known him, I have come to appreciate
more fully his fatherhood.*

*My family has been extremely supportive as well. I have been very
blessed because I know this is not always the case. My family is growing in their faith everyday, and my pursuit of a priestly vocation is both
influenced by them and influences them as well. I have also benefited
greatly through Fr. Paul Sullivan, the vocation director of the Diocese of
Phoenix. He was very helpful and kept in contact with me all the while
I was at Franciscan."* **J. Michael Villanueva—First Year Theology—
Anthem, AZ—[Diocese of Phoenix]**

Prayer is the source of our spiritual energy At the Josephinum,
seminarians gather daily for morning and evening prayer, and start
each morning with a meditation on the Word of God. Scripture is
the privileged source of all our prayer and, like the early Church, we
ponder God's Word in our hearts daily.

Our Eucharistic prayer is the center of our day. We participate
at Mass and frequent Eucharistic Adoration, to emphasize the intimate, personal quality Our Lord wants for our prayer.

We deepen our recollection and our discipleship through spiritual reading, study, and times set apart in an atmosphere of recollection and silence. Each month we set aside one day for retreat, and every year we make a week-long retreat. But often enough, it is the good example of others that gives us that first nudge:

"There are five in my family: my dad, mom and my two sisters. I am the middle child and the only boy.

A priest that was at my home parish for 12 years, is pretty much is the reason I am in seminary. I saw how he was happy and enjoyed the life of a priest and I was drawn to it. He helped me answer so many questions I had about the priesthood. My grandma played a hidden role in my decision, it was because of her always telling me how she thought that I would make a great priest that I really took the thought seriously.

In fifth grade I began to be an altar server. I like being up at the altar helping instead of just in the pews. Jump now to Junior year of high school when we were told to start applying for colleges. I had no idea what I was going to do. My grandma was a very holy person in my eyes and she always told me that she thought I would be a good priest. She passed away suddenly, and a month later, I was thinking about what she had told me about seeing me as a priest. I decided to really look into this vocation. The biggest help was I wrote a single spaced page of questions that I had about the priesthood and sent it to one of the best priests I knew at the time and he sent a letter back answering all of my questions. I then went and met with him and it was then that I really felt called to start the process of entering seminary.

I hadn't told any of my family even my parents that I was considering the priesthood. I met and asked questions without alerting my family so that I wouldn't get their hopes up if I decided this was not what I was meant to do. But after I really thought this was what I wanted to do the first person I told was my mom. She had just asked were I was going to go to college and I told her I was still figuring it out, then we left to go to my grandpa's house and I decided to tell her as soon as we pulled out of the drive. She was very happy and supportive, especially when I told he all that I had done in the past few months to figure out if this was what I should do. Next was my dad and my two sisters. They really were not surprised, I think they figured it out when mom was crying tears of joy as I started to tell them the story. My biggest memory was telling my mom's side which is very large, around 50 people. It was Thanksgiving dinner at our house and we always go around and say what we are thankful for, well right before that I stood up and told everyone that I was going to enter seminary to study to become a priest. I brought my grandpa to tears, which I had never really seen him do, because of how happy he was about my decision and since his wife, my grandma was the one who always told me that she thought I would be a great priest.

I was very surprised when I received the application process, it was much larger than I thought it would be. It took me a long time to complete due to the needed material. There was a physical, blood tests, psychological exam, finger printing, FBI background check, letters of recommendation, autobiography, records of sacraments and a few other things. It was much more involved than I thought. All my family was very supportive. Most of my friends were as well, especially my friends that were Catholic. Some friends didn't understand why I wanted to become a priest and give up the possibility of getting married and having kids. But overall their reactions were of support and happiness.

I visited the Josephinum for one day in February of 2011 during the semester before I came to the Josephinum. I was surprised at how big the campus itself was. I really didn't know a whole lot about it before I came here, just a few little things. My biggest impression was how nice everyone was, they were all very welcoming and helpful, answering any questions which we might have. It was also interesting to have all the different dioceses there and being able to interact with the men from many dioceses." Zach Brown—Third Year College—Attica, Ohio—[Diocese of Toledo]

It is not all prayer and silence at the Josephinum! We take time every day for appropriate recreation. Many visitors have remarked on the spirit of joy which permeates our community. We have fun in many different ways. We enjoy each others presence at meals each day, but our interests and hobbies vary widely: from watching movies to exercising, participating in inter-mural and inter-seminary sports, to playing musical instruments or taking long hikes in nature. Our free time is used to relax, enjoy each other, deepen our understanding of the culture in which we live, and grow in personal freedom and integrity. In its most authentic sense, free time is a time for "re-creation."

So, as you begin your discernment, what kind of a time frame should you set? On the one hand, you don't want to be stuck in indecision, waffling back and forth endlessly; but rushing isn't helpful either.

A reasonable time line is a year to two years, although there are reasons for discernment to last longer. Why so long? To put it briefly, time is needed to research, to pray, to benefit from spiritual direction, to grow in your relationship with God, and to test your vocational choice. This is a lifetime decision you're making!

Even after weighing the pros and cons intellectually, you might need space and time to understand how your heart was moved. Did something about the priesthood particularly attract you, or even repulse you? Why? Did you feel at peace with one thing more than another? Sometime, it may seem like forever, but be steadfast and of good heart! Consider the lengthy experience of one seminarian as he approaches his ordination:

"Before I entered seminary I had lived with my parents. I have a sister and two brothers, all of them happily married. I have four nieces and a nephew.

I received my call at the age of eight. I entered the seminary three weeks before I turned thirty-five. That long! When I lived in Mexico, my pastor was an old priest from the south of the country, who influenced me greatly. He was a man who gave his life to God and his people. So much so that when he died he was buried in our home town, far away from his own lands and family.

The application and acceptance process was providential. My application process went as smooth as butter. It was quite inclusive, as my brothers here have already pointed out. But all the doors 'opened wide before me.' Even the application to join the Josephinum was a breeze.

I had told my mother that I was joining the seminary just two weeks before they left to go to California. I had already told my friends, relatives and even my neighbors. But I had not yet the courage to tell my parents. When I told my mom about my desire to enter the seminary she said in a very calm voice "You are old enough to make your own decision. May God bless you." Overall, they received the news with much joy and happiness. I was a bit sad because I was leaving my people behind to travel to Ohio. I wouldn't be spending much time with my nieces, my friends, my co-workers, my parents. There were a couple of farewell parties held at the places I used to attend and assist them during Mass. My pastor and my parishioners threw a huge farewell party as well.

I knew nothing of the Josephinum! However, when I first met with my Director of Vocations, and he mentioned the PCJ, somehow I knew I was coming here. I was thrilled, considering that for years, the farthest I had traveled had been to Houston. The fact that I was going to be sent to Ohio was somewhat scary. But I surrendered completely to the will of God. So much so that when I met with Msgr. Langsfeld, who was then the Rector, and he told me that I was going to begin as a Pre-Theology undergraduate and not as a Pre-Theology graduate student (eight years to ordination instead of six), I told him that it was fine with me. After all I was already in the seminary! It did not matter to me whether I would have to be here eight or more years. However, I did ask him to inform my Director of Vocations, though, since there were two more years being added to my formation plan. The diocese readily agreed.

I arrived at the Josephinum on a Sunday afternoon. It was cloudy and quite humid too. But the place was magnificent! It took me some time before I learned to get around the buildings. The sun does not shine too often in Columbus, so I had some trouble situating myself (north, south, east, etc). With the grace of God I have made myself at home. It has been an incredible journey for me and for my loved ones."
Jesse Garza—Third Year Theology—Mission, TX—[Diocese of Brownsville]

A common thread in all of these seminarian's stories is prayer. Bring your personal experiences to prayer. Does what you see in the seminary fit with what you know about yourself, or hope for yourself? How did you feel when/ if you had the opportunity to visit the Josephinum? At peace? Energized? Joyful?

How do you feel about the experience once you have returned to every day life?

Vocation Directors are trained in the ways of discernment and can help you to recognize the ways God is working in your life. Your director will be understanding and help you to discover a sense of freedom in your discernment. But the decision you make is yours, not your director's. Ideally, a director will encourage you to examine the many options you have, to help you become more aware of your own motivations, and to bring your experiences to prayer.

You may find it helpful to talk over your discernment with other people your trust. Your parents, pastor, other priests and even trusted and trustworthy friends can help us to see things about ourselves that we may not. Consider the experiences of the last student profiled in this chapter:

> *"My parents always required us to go to Mass on a weekly basis and encouraged prayer at the meals we had together, and when we were little we would pray before going to bed. As my brothers and I grew older, we prayed less and less together, and Mass became less of a priority. At the same time, I was becoming more involved in the Church, so I became the one who would persuade the rest of the family to make the effort to go to Mass and pray together. At family functions, I am still the one who leads the prayer before meals. My twin brother also served with me during Mass until we entered high school, although I continued to serve.*
>
> *My grandfather was a very influential figure in my faith life because of his quiet devotion and witness to being Catholic. He was an altar boy growing up, and many times would tell me stories of serving at his home parish. He also raised all six of his children in the faith, and was very proud when I began to serve. In addition, my great uncle is a bishop. Although I did not get to see him regularly, it was very powerful to know that someone in my family had given his life in service to the Church.*
>
> *I first began to discern a religious vocation when I was invited by my pastor to be an altar server in the third grade. This helped me grow in my understanding of and appreciation for the Mass and the priesthood. In sixth grade, I had two wonderful catechists for CCD at my home parish who sparked my interest in Catholic devotional prayer, the*

lives of the saints, and theology. Their enthusiasm and knowledge of the faith helped me to become more interested, and eventually I began to study the faith on my own. Friends and family members took notice of my interest, and many people asked about and encouraged me to think about the priesthood, especially as I entered high school. I prayed about this decision frequently, but ultimately decided to first go to Catholic University of America to study theology and philosophy. I wanted to have an environment that would foster my vocational discernment, and CUA was that and more. At CUA, I was introduced to a broader experience of what it meant to be Catholic, and I was also introduced to many other kinds of religious vocations besides diocesan priests. As I concluded my time at CUA, I was much more free and educated in making the decision to enter the seminary for the Diocese of Columbus.

Fr. Jan Sullivan, who was my pastor for 12 years, was very influential in my discernment process. He taught me about the beauty of the liturgy, the roses and thorns of priestly life, and always made himself available to answer any of my questions. Additionally, I encountered a number of other priests, religious, and lay people while studying at The Catholic University of America who augmented my understanding of the priesthood and the treasures of the Catholic intellectual tradition. It was really after encountering the profound beauty of the Catholic faith, intellectually and sacramentally, that I knew I was ready to apply to seminary.

It was not an easy task to go through the admissions process while I was a college student, especially because I was eight hours away from my home diocese. During Christmas Break my senior year, I had an interview with the vocations director and began the application process by filling out questionnaires, scheduling appointments with my doctors, and gathering my sacramental records. When I was home for Spring Break, I went through a psychological assessment. After returning to

CUA, I went to the student health center for the remaining health and blood tests. Shortly thereafter, I finished my eight-page autobiography and the many short essays required in the application to the diocese and the Josephinum.

My family has always been very supportive of my vocational discernment. It was no huge surprise to any of my extended or immediate family members when I decided to apply to seminary. Now that I am in seminary, they continue to show their support by visiting me regularly, especially for Sunday Mass and brunch. Since I spent the last four years in Washington, D.C., this has been a great privilege to be able to study for the priesthood in such close proximity to my family. My twin brother lives in Columbus as well, and is able to visit often.

When I was accepted, I was overwhelmed by the amount of support that I received from family, friends, and people whom I had never expected to hear from. It was a very joyous time for me, to know that I would soon be taking a very significant step in my vocational journey.

Because I grew up in the Diocese of Columbus, I have known of the Josephinum for a long time. I don't think I will ever forget the feeling of peace that I experienced on my first visit. I remember distinctly the prayerfulness, the smell of incense, the beauty of the architecture, all of which captivated my senses. I had an intuition, even though I was just beginning my discernment, that I would one day return there. This past fall, that intuition was realized. Although many small things have changed, I was happy to find the Josephinum no less captivating than when I first visited nine years earlier." **Brett Garland—Second Year Pre-Theology—Washington CH, Ohio—[Diocese of Columbus]**

In summation, always keep in mind that your vocation is not just God's invitation, but also how you respond to that invitation. Each year, dozens of young Catholic men just like you – nervous, worried, even frightened— take that vital first step and approach their pastor, a trusted priest-friend, or their Diocesan Vocation Director for advice and assistance. Remember, if God is really calling you to the priesthood, he will always wait until you are ready to accept!

2 THE HOUSE THAT JOSEPH BUILT

"[Coming to the Josephinum] was the strangest feeling. I was in a strange place, but there's something about discovering that you are in a community of like-minded men. Only God could construct a place, that in your first days, all at once feels foreign and just like home. My official house job is maintenance crew, which means I help move heavy things. Unofficially, since I am good with electronic repair, I've been helping to repair things which break... a TV set in the pub, a hard drive with a burned controller board, an iPad with water damage, and soon a BIOS chip swap on a MacBook." **Gordon Mott— First Year Pre-Theology—Columbus, OH—[Diocese of Columbus]**

Suppose that, just like Gordon, you have prayerfully completed a period of discernment. You've consulted with your family, discussed the matter with your pastor and diocesan vocation director, completed all the necessary paperwork, undergone all the necessary assessments, and —at long last – the much awaited phone call or letter arrives. You're in! And your bishop has assigned you to the Pontifical College Josephinum, in far off (well, maybe) Columbus, Ohio. And all you know about Columbus is that it's where the Ohio State Buckeyes play. Perhaps you too might some day find yourself rooting for the Buckeyes, especially when they play their arch-rivals, The University of Michigan. But what is this "Pontifical College Josephinum" anyway?

Our story begins in the early 19th century. A young German, John William Jessing of Stadtlohn in Westphalia, and Anna Maria Schlusemann married and soon had three children.

First among them was John Joseph, born on November 17, 1836. A daughter, Wilhelmina Frances followed in 1839 and a second boy, Bernard Anthony William followed in August 1841. But in late 1840, even before the birth of Bernard, John William Jessing died, leaving a very young family nearly destitute.

As a boy, young Joseph Jessing (as he was known to family and associates) worked in a print shop to provide for his mother and two siblings. The young boy devoted what little spare time he had to reading and study. When he grew to manhood, Jessing enlisted in the Prussian army, an organization known for its severe training and discipline. He rose to the rank of quartermaster sergeant, proving himself a successful fighter as well as a skilled logistician during the First and Second wars with Denmark. Joseph was decorated by William I of Prussia for bravery at the Battle of Dybbøl. He earned many decorations and medals for his service in the Seventh Westphalian Artillery, but despite all these military achievements, Joseph's dream of the priesthood remained his true ambition.

In 1867, Jessing left his home in Westphalia to pursue his life-long vocation to the Roman Catholic priesthood. Unbeknownst to him then, this was the first of many steps he would take toward the founding of an orphanage, a college and a seminary in the United States.

Arriving in Ohio, he began his studies at Mount Saint Mary's Seminary in Cincinnati in 1868. He was ordained to the priesthood by the first bishop of Columbus, Sylvester Rosecrans, at St. Patrick Pro Cathedral in Columbus on July 16, 1870, and was assigned to

Sacred Heart Church in the town of Pomeroy, in the hardscrabble coal fields of southeastern Ohio.

Soon after arriving at Sacred Heart, Father Jessing became deeply concerned about the many sons of miners orphaned after the deaths of their fathers in the mines. With the assistance of the Brothers of Saint Francis, he provided these needy children with shelter, food, and schooling. This work led to his establishing the Saint Joseph Orphan Asylum, funded primarily through a German-language newspaper, "The Ohio" (later called "Ohio Waisenfreund" meaning "Ohio Orphan's Friend"), with Father Jessing, a skilled lithographer, as chief writer and publisher. Father Jessing used the proceeds from the small but popular newspaper to fund his work with the orphans so that it would be self-sustaining.

In 1877, Father Jessing wrote to Bishop Rosecrans asking permission to bring his newspaper and the orphan's asylum to a larger city. In that letter, he explained that he needed to be closer to the railroad in order to better distribute his paper. Since he wanted the work to be self-sustaining, he also discussed an industrial school that he wanted to start in connection with the orphan's asylum where boys could learn a trade to support themselves as adults.

Bishop Rosecrans approved Father Jessing's plan, and the newspaper and orphan's asylum were moved to Columbus later that year. Besides the industrial school, Father Jessing started various enterprises for the orphans including the Josephinum Church Furniture Company where the boys could be taught a trade.

When several older boys expressed a desire to study for the priesthood, Father Jessing advertised in his paper that he would sponsor two boys who wished to become priests but who lacked the financial means to do so.

Of the forty applicants, Jessing accepted twenty-three and the first academic classes began on September 1, 1888. In memory of the original St. Joseph's Orphanage, this seminary was called, in Latin, the Collegium Josephinum or St. Joseph's College.

Fast-forward one hundred twenty-five years. Just for a moment, imagine yourself in the shoes of a young aspirant chatting with a few old hands as they guide you around the product of Father Jessing's vision:

"Columbus is nice. Everything I need is not very far away. The city is to get around in, and there are lots of good and cheap restaurants nearby. It's the biggest city I have ever been in for any long period of time, but I enjoy going out to the Highbanks metro park just up High Street and walking around out there.

At first I was overwhelmed by the intensity of the schedule. The days are jam packed with classes, prayer, meetings, etc. It took a few days to set up a personal schedule that worked for me. Once I got that figured out, I really began to enjoy my classes and the prayer and just take everything in that was going on around me.

In New Mexico, the sun shines pretty much every day. Here, not so much. I had never needed an umbrella back home, but that was one of the first things I bought when I got here. It's more humid here than I'm used to. In the winter, it's colder too. Over Christmas break, my car battery froze. I had never even thought about that happening until I was here. I do like how there are lots of trees and green grass every-where. It's a nice change compared to the desert of New Mexico.
Brian Aerts—First Year Pre-Theology—San Antonio, NM— [Diocese of Santa Fe]

22

"I was enthusiastic myself when I visited my first time a few months before coming here. I was even more excited to come here August of 2012 when I had orientation which was amazing!

Virginia is warmer compared to here, the weather just makes me appreciate home more. I experienced my first day below freezing this year and I don't remember the last time it got that cold in Virginia. Its not as busy as Arlington and DC area, which is nice in some ways but I always like doing new things and there isn't as much in Columbus attractions-wise like DC." **Blaise Radel—Second Year College—Arlington, Va—[Diocese of Arlington]**

"When I first arrived, I thought to myself "What did I get myself into?" This place has so many halls and doors to get confused with. The guys here are great; brothers that I never had before, being the only boy among two sisters. At least, since I am from Ohio this weather is what I am use to, although there's a little less snow than farther north. It is very nice, a little noisier than what I am use to living in the country or in a small town. There is everything around that someone would need, shopping, food, movies, games, etc.

The rooms are very nice, I like the personal room with a joining room sharing a half bath. Classrooms serve their purpose, most of them are the same. Our chapels are nice; I enjoy St. Pius the most. It's the easiest place to pray since it is only down six steps from my hallway. There are good paths to walk on too, either in the woods or on the driveways." **Zach Brown—Third Year College—Attica, Ohio—[Diocese of Toledo]**

"I was pretty anxious upon first getting here. I was, for the first time, held to a very rigid schedule and surrounded by all new people for the

second consecutive year (since I attended my freshman year of college at a college where I also knew nobody.)

Columbus, at least my first year, seemed to have a permanent gray sky that I wasn't used to at home. I think we have the most diversity in activities Columbus has to offer (besides maybe OSU.) I still brag to my friends at home about our brand new gym floor, our bowling alley and our heated pool. The campus as well is gorgeous, offering extensive woodlands, a small pond with a pathway around it, and several beautiful views of our impressive architecture against the backdrop of fields.

I am glad to have a brand new room since they were renovated during my second semester here. At first I was simply thrilled to have a place to myself, and it got even better when they added shelf space, wooden floors and provided me with a brand new mattress. Although at times it feels cramped, visitors always assure me that I am blessed with what I am given and I believe them." **Joey Collopy—Fourth Year College—Ft. Thomas, Ky.—[Diocese of Covington]**

"I was pleasantly surprised at how easily I got to know all of the seminary brothers and how quickly I got a sense of the place. I was also pleasantly surprised at how enjoyable seminary life seemed, contrasting my initial dread at going back to undergraduate studies after 7 1/2 years of undergraduate and graduate study and then being at work in the professional world (no papers due there!) I was overwhelmed by the shifting schedules, corrections, and endless rivers of paper that flowed across the day board in those first few days and weeks.

While it does get cold in the winter in Nashville and sometimes rainy and dark, it is, of course, much colder up here. I'm okay with this, but the one thing that really gives me trouble up here is what many of us out-of-townees call the 'permacloud'. It is sometimes nearly unbearable how long one can go without seeing the sun. The positive side of all this is that going back home to Nashville is usually a sigh of bliss.

The facilities are old, of course, but generally acceptable; my room on the 4th-floor is nice. I have very few complaints. The main building is beautiful." **Richard Childress—Second Year Pre-Theology— Nashville,Tn.—[Diocese of Nashville]**

To ensure that the Josephinum would continue to educate priests to serve German-speaking emigres after his death, Father Jessing asked that the fledgling institution be placed under the protection of the Holy See. Pope Leo XIII granted the request in 1892, thus making the Pontifical College Josephinum the only pontifical seminary outside of Italy. From that time to the present, the institution has been under the direction of the Congregation for Seminaries and Institutes of Study, with the Apostolic Nuncio to the United States (the Pope's ambassador) as its Chancellor. The seminary though, is financially independent from both the Holy See and the Diocese of Columbus. The first class, consisting of six seminarians was ordained to the priesthood in June 1899. Monsignor Jessing was privileged to witnessed this before he died a few months later in early November 1899.

Originally established on East Main Street, just a short distance from the Ohio Statehouse and several rail termini, in 1931, Father Jessing's seminary, the Josephinum, moved to its present location in Worthington, Ohio, eleven miles north of Columbus on a nearly one-hundred acre campus. The Josephinum continues to inspire seminarians even in in its one hundred and twenty-fifth year of service to the Church:

"My room is small, but cozy. I had lived in a travel trailer for all four years of college, so I am used to the small space. These rooms have

25

recently been remodeled, so the furniture is good, and there is lots of shelf space and storage. The chapels are great. My favorite is St. Rose of Lima because it's a small, intimate kind of place. It's a nice place to get away for a few minutes and pray. The classrooms and other facilities are great. Everything is very close and easy to get to once you figure out the floor plan of the buildings." **[Brian Aerts]**

"I think my favorite chapel is St. Rose of Lima because of the calm quiet atmosphere. But the chapels here in general are very nice but especially St. Rose and St. Joseph. It's awesome to have my own room since I shared mine with four other brothers at home. The Classrooms are much nicer than the ones I had in high school. I love our gym, especially the basketball court." **[Blaise Radel]**

"I keep my window open all the time in my room for fresh air and a cooling draft. The library classrooms are a bit warm and so are some of the chapels in the summer. But the new HVAC in the chapels is helping that issue. A brick building is tough to heat and cool, so you just deal with the warm / cold rooms." **Mitchel Roman—First Year Pre-Theology—Empire MI [Diocese of Gaylord]**

"Once the heat is on it stays on even if you turn your radiator off! Some parts of the building stay really hot while others get cold. Then in the summer it gets really hot because all you can do is to move the hot air using fans. But overall it is okay. Because of the major reconstruction of U.S. Route 23, which abuts the property, the State just tore down several trees which had made this place look so cool. By the same respect, taking the trees out removed a noise block so now the traffic noise is much louder. The real pain is coming in and out of Campusview Boulevard's traffic light; sometimes it works right, but at others times you sit there for three cycles of the light before you finally get a green light to go. Most of us have to experience the pain of the construction and

will never experience the end goal of the project because we will graduate and perhaps move to a different seminary before it is finished." [Zach **Brown]**

The buildings on this new property were designed and constructed solely for the Pontifical College Josephinum by Frank A. Ludewig, a registered architect of St. Louis, Missouri. The main structure is predominantly gothic; and while architects are sometimes accused of building castles in the air, Mr. Ludewig had the unusual experience of actually being responsible for the restoration and reconstruction of a castle near his birthplace in Nijmegen, overlooking the River Waal. While the the Castle at Wychen in the Netherlands can rightly be called his European masterpiece, the Pontifical College Josephinum is rightly regarded as the capstone of his entire career. He died in September 1940, in Holland Michigan.

There are presently five major structures on this approximately one hundred-acre property. These include the main seminary building, containing administrative offices, classrooms and lecture halls as well as the residence for the students of the graduate School of Theology, dining and recreational facilities; the College Academic Center, and the Pope John Paul II Education Center, housing the A.T. Wehrle Memorial Library. This property also contains the Monsignor John Joseph Jessing Center, an outreach facility for the institution, which was constructed in 1938 as the Seminary's library, and renewed and re-focused in 1982. The property also houses the undergraduate College of Liberal Arts in a building constructed in 1957-59, a recreation building constructed concurrently, and the original workshops and powerhouse.

Through the wisdom and prudence of the Board of Trustees, these buildings have been continuously maintained, and the architectural detail conserved by subsequent generations. There is striking congruity between photographs taken on the day of dedication in 1931 and those taken recently. Major restoration and conservation of the slate roof and other elements was completed in 2008, and revitalization of the undergraduate residence and classroom building was completed in 2013.

The main building, which measures 600 feet in length (East-West) by 350 feet wide (North-South) contains terrazzo floors in areas of public access, as well as hand-crafted inlaid woodwork throughout the building. Elements of the building are connected by enclosed brick cloisters in the European fashion.

Each of the four chapels at the Josephinum contains original stained-glass windows, of which those of St. Joseph's Oratory, the chapel for the School of Theology, are perhaps most striking. Windows on the north and south sides represent scenes from the life of Christ, while those in the front of the oratory represent the four priestly virtues of Prudence, Justice, Fortitude and Temperance. Paintings on the walls depict interpretations of St. John's Gospel, and were completed in 1931 by Gerhard Lamers, a native of Cleves, Westphalia, also near the Dutch border, and whose work also graces St. Mary's Church in Columbus and many other Roman Catholic Churches in Ohio.

The academic structure changed over time during the 1940s and 1950s from the "six-six" format to four years of high school, four years of college, and four years of theology/seminary (though the distinctions were gradual and unclear.) The first official College commencement occurred in June 1953; the College and Recreation buildings were dedicated in 1958; while the high school closed in 1967.

For the first few decades of its existence, the Josephinum continued its mission and focused its efforts on educating priests to work with the large population of German immigrants in the United States. After World War I, that focus shifted to preparing priests for dioceses that lack their own seminary. In recent years, the Josephinum has been blessed with a number of candidates from Eastern Europe, Asia, and Africa who come to the seminary to be educated for service in their native lands.

A Roman Catholic Seminary – particularly prior to the Second Vatican Council (1962-65) – is and was much different than a secular or religious college. In the earliest years of the North High Street location, students arrived on campus in early September, and, except for rare periods of absence – medical appointments, participation in extraordinary religious activities at the downtown cathedral or the like— remained on campus at all times until the Christmas holidays. Once they returned in January, they faced a long, and often bleak, period of "confinement" until summer vacation. The institution was completely self-contained, with dormitories, refectory, chapels, classrooms, library, and surprisingly varied recreational facilities located within the campus confines.

Daily life was much more austere however. Msgr. Leonard Fick, writing on the occasion of the Josephinum's centennial in 1988, writes of one institutional treasurer who guided the seminary through the darkest days of the depression:

"Father William J. Spiegel, it may be said without fear of contradiction, was an able collector of the coin of the realm, and a brilliant distributor and conservator of these monies. For Father Spiegel green in any denomination was a color most pleasing to the Lord."

"The fact that he got the Josephinum through the difficult years of the depression is a tribute to his tireless efforts and his financial ability and his charm. It is generally accepted knowledge that for six months of the school year he provided food for the entire Josephinum family on an outlay of $.15 per person per day. This involved early Saturday morning trips to the farmers' market, driving bargains that the farmers themselves found difficult to comprehend. Occasionally an alumnus would send him fifty bushels of potatoes, or ex-student one hundred pounds of Navy beans. But there were no epidemics of any kind and the students were happy and content."

That contentment with refectory offerings seems to continue to this day:

"The food served is good. Of course, there are some things served that aren't my favorite, but I'm usually satisfied." **[Brian Aerts]**

"I really enjoy the food here, we are well fed. That is probably the main reason that I chose the dining room and food committee as my house job." **[Blaise Radel]**

"It was better than I thought. I heard war stories of other college food from bigger universities. It has had its bad and good days, but overall it is good enough to eat." **[Zach Brown]**

"The food is good and many options have been made. This current year the kitchen staff has been providing healthy options for all who want to stay healthy and fit." **Dean Carson—First Year Theology— Louisville, OH—[Diocese of Columbus]**

"I personally enjoy the food in the refectory. Sometimes you get a miss when they try to make Indian food (or is it Chinese, I can't

30

really tell.) Its always a great night when they pull out the prime rib (if that is what it's called) because it's just a huge hunk of meat that looks like it was just sliced from the side of the cow. Lunch is always a favorite of mine with all the varieties. The staff do a great job of getting creative with the dressings, condiments, salads and soups."
Estevan Wetzel—Fourth Year College—Phoenix, AZ.—[Diocese of Phoenix]

Monsignor Fick continues: "Here is a sampling of the rules indicated the Teutonic character of the Josephinum's founder:

- The students will say the rosary in common on all those days on which there is no second Holy Mass or other special devotions;

- Should any dispute arise among the students, it should be at once reported to the Very Rev. Rector for settlement;

- No student is allowed to leave the premises of the Josephinum without the Very Rev. Rector's Permission;

- Smoking or any other use of tobacco is strictly forbidden;

- All letters sent or received by the students must pass through the hands of the Very Rev. Rector. The students are not allowed to receive books, pamphlets, or periodicals of any kind;

- The students are forbidden to keep money in their possession;

- From the first to the 15th of each month, the English language, and from the 16th to the end of the month, the German language, will be exclusively use in conversation;

31

- No one should take athletic exercises when wearing his Sunday clothes. All rude games, especially baseball, are strictly prohibited to the students;

- Students that will be found habitually to transgress these rules shall be liable to dismissal.

It is difficult to fathom the founder's distaste for baseball. Perhaps, like those who have come after him, his heart had been repeatedly been broken by our beloved Cleveland Indians. There is one innovation, though which no doubt would warm the Teutonic heart of Monsignor Jessing. The Josephinum houses a modern *Kegelbahn* (bowling alley) for seminarians' enjoyment:

> *"I have worked the bowling alley both years I've been here so far, apparently due to my having worked as an HVAC technician (and therefore being mechanically-knowledgeable and inclined.) I turn on all the machines, supervise the safety of any bowlers that show up, fix mechanical problems with the machines when a lane jams, and then close up and occasionally clean the machines in back. "* **[Richard Childress]**

> *"The cardio room is very nice, except for the fact that it is under the library and you have to go through public areas to get to it. The gym was nice before the new floor was installed, but now it is <u>really</u> nice; it looks like a real gym. The bowling alley is cool as well; not many seminaries can boast of a bowling alley in their basement. The softball field also provides some great times and memories during the fall and spring."* **[Zach Brown]**

As described by Monsignor Fick, the daily schedule in 1888 was likewise rather rigid:

5:30 AM	Rising and morning prayers
6:30 AM	Holy Mass
7:30 AM	Breakfast
8 AM – 10 AM	Study Time
10 AM - 10:30 AM	Recess
10:30 AM - Noon	Dinner, Recreation
2 PM - 3:30 PM	Study Time
3:30 PM - 4 PM	Recess
4:30 PM - 6 PM	Study Time
6 PM - 7:30 PM	Supper, Recreation
7:30 PM	Evening Prayers
7:45 PM - 9 PM	Study Time
9:30 PM	Retiring

Students were prohibited from owning or operating motor vehicles until the mid-1960s, and, in any event, the then-remote location, two miles or more north of the center of the small village of Worthington, forced students to look inward for emotional and spiritual support. It is not unusual, then, that the emotional attachment to "The Joss" was and is extraordinarily strong among ordained and non-ordained alumni alike. The Josephinum was, at once, home, school, church, "restaurant" and recreation center for those fortunate enough to survive the rigorous entrance procedures and taxing curriculum. But seminarians can be adventuresome and energetic and the gothic architecture of the Josephinum (described by one contemporary seminarian as being "Hogwarts without Hermionie") can provide a source of temptation to the adventurer. One wandering seminarian, [whose name has been changed to protect him from the wrath of the facilities-management staff] relates:

"In the powerhouse, on the top floor, there is a creepy area that seems to be old dorm rooms. Myself and another seminarian wandered up

33

there once and found the place to be a mess. The only thing that was a bit eerie is that there is just a croquet set and a portrait of a man and woman up there.

If you want an adventure, going through the powerhouse tunnel is always a way to do something different. When my parents came for family weekend I actually took them through it". **[Urban Explorer]**

Since 1899, when six of the original twenty-three students were ordained, more than 1500 priests have received their education at the Pontifical College Josephinum; and more 350 graduates of the College of Liberal Arts have completed their studies for ordination at other seminaries.

The Pontifical College Josephinum has long enjoyed the reputation within the Roman Catholic Church as the *West Point on the Olentangy*, recognizing the academic rigor of both its undergraduate and graduate programs. Remarkably, given its relatively small size, eleven graduates and three former rectors have been elevated to the hierarchy of the Church:

- Bernard Cardinal Law (Cardinal Archbishop Emeritus of Boston)
- Most Rev. Robert Baker (Bishop of Birmingham, AL)
- Most Rev. Leroy Matthiesen (Bishop of Amarillo, TX d.2010)
- Most Rev. Thomas Tschope (Retired Bishop of Dallas, TX)
- Most Rev. David Fellhauer (Bishop of Victoria, TX
- Most Rev. David Ricken, (Bishop of Green Bay WI)

- Most Rev. Blaise Cupich   (Bishop of Spokane WA)
- Most Rev. Ronald Herzog   (Bishop of Alexandria, LA)
- Most Rev. Alexander Sample   (Bishop of Portland, OR)
- Most Rev. Thomas Olmsted   (Bishop of Phoenix AZ)
- Most Rev. Robert Lynch   (Bishop of St. Petersburg, FL)
- Most Rev. William Skylstad   (Retired Bishop of Spokane, WA)
- Most Rev. Earl Boyea   (Bishop of Lansing, MI)
- Most Rev. John Brunghardt   (Bishop of Dodge City, KS)

Since 1931, each of the prelates listed above, and over 1400 other priests have completed their education at the current location of the Pontifical College Josephinum. Additionally, nearly 2000 other young men have completed degrees in philosophy or theology, and, having decided not to seek ordination, have gone on to successful careers in education, commerce and industry.

Over the years, seminarians have benefited from daily contact with "the greats" – priests who had given their lives for the formation of the clergy: Monsignor Nicholas Pinter, who taught classical languages for fifty-five years; Monsignor Anthony Kleinshmidt, who spent over forty years as the Josephinum librarian, Monsignor Leonard J. Fick, who spent over forty years as professor of English and Literature. Long serving faculty and staff now incumbent include Peter G. Veracka, Associate Professor of Theology and Director of Library Services, thirty-eight years; Dr. David J. De Leonardis, Associate Professor and Academic Dean and Director of College Academic Formation, thirty years; Dr. Alma Amell, Professor and Director of Hispanic Formation, twenty-nine years and Father Joseph

A. Murphy SJ, STD Associate Professor and Director of Human Formation, Theology, sixteen years. The dedication and loyalty of the faculty and staff, regardless of their term of service, bears witness to the extraordinary character of the Josephinum – the House that Joseph built.

3 LIFE IN COMMUNITY

"Living with 200 other guys has its challenges, but it also comes with many unexpected graces. Many of us are stubborn and argumentative, which makes for interesting dinner conversations, but we are also all united by a common goal: growth in holiness. There are times when I wonder what I have gotten myself into, but more often than not I am edified by the daily interactions and conversations I have with my brother seminarians. When it is all said and done, we are here to support each other in our discernment of the priesthood. Sometimes that support comes in the form of spending time in the pub or playing soccer, and sometimes it comes in the form of praying night prayer together or studying philosophy late into the night." **Brett Garland—Second Year Pre-Theology—Washington CH,Ohio—[Diocese of Columbus]**

One frequently-noted dichotomy in priestly formation is this: Priests are trained and educated in large fraternal communities, yet generally reside in rectories housing only one or two priests living together. While efficiency and economies of scale play a part in this process, the Josephinum, as well as the forty-six other accredited seminaries in the United States have a deeper rationale, both psychological and theological, for maintaining this tradition:

We form future priests the same way that Jesus formed his first disciples and apostles.

When a newly accepted seminarian first arrives at the Pontifical College Josephinum, and throughout his tenure here, he soon comes to understand that a very real sense of priestly community marks this seminary. In a very real way it emulates the way Jesus taught his first disciples, through dialog, exhortation and by example.

The Josephinum is committed to fostering the human, spiritual, intellectual and pastoral formation of future priests who will serve the needs of the faithful throughout North America and indeed, the world.

The essential work of the Josephinum takes place in this context of our community. A seminarian's personal growth and character development progresses hand-in-hand with his deepening spiritual life. In a very real sense, the Josephinum is a school of human virtue: A place where growth in honesty, integrity, intellectual rigor, hard work and tolerance thrive. It is a place where the common good unites with solidarity and discipline, and does so in the context of great good humor and manly recreation. It is a school of spiritual work where men come, imbued with the virtues of faith, hope, and charity.

It is at the Josephinum that seminarians develop those lasting relationships and skills of dialogue which are critical to the healthy interpersonal relationships they will need as priests. At the Josephinum, a seminarian's study has two primary focal points: the life of community and a personal journey to internalize the values of spiritual life and the integration of those lessons with intellectual and pastoral formation. This interplay between community and individual group lies at the very heart of priestly formation.

The experience of seminary community life plays a significant role in the personal and spiritual growth of our seminarians. Each level of seminary life, from the collegiate through Pre-Theology to the theologate, shapes the seminarian in a particular way. But at every level the community functions in similar ways. The give-and-take between those who share the priesthood as a common vocation sets the right context for formation. Such interaction provides mutual support, promotes tolerance and fraternal correction, and gives an opportunity for the development of leadership and talent among our seminarians. It motivates them to develop a sense of self-sacrifice and a spirit of willing and thoughtful collaboration. It provides a secure and peaceful context where the qualities necessary for those called to the priesthood, — emotional maturity, personal faith, moral integrity and social concern — can be nurtured and demonstrated. Led by experienced and dedicated faculty, these seminarians form the heart of the faith community which is the Pontifical College Josephinum.

Consider the earliest experiences of five seminarians we met in Chapters One and Two:

"It was definitely a little daunting at the threshold. As I pulled onto campus, I remember thinking, 'All of these guys are going to be ultra-pious and precious, and therefore easily offended. I'm going to have to watch my step here.' Then Brian Seiler, who was on the orientation team, helped me move in, and then I also remembered my friend Andy Forsythe was here. And so I realized that in some cases real men do go to seminary. This was a fact that I came to see more and more as I got to know more seminarian brothers. And that's the best part of this experience. If it weren't for the fraternity you can find here, I don't know who wouldn't discern out within a year. I've made several good friends here, and many more good acquaintances, and can honestly say at this point that there's no one here I can't stand, however much I may prefer others' company to that of certain persons. The pressures of the school-year apply friction which expresses itself in the community, and

we have house triumphs and sufferings, but each semester is just long enough for us to work some of this out and not get tired of living with 199 other men." [Richard Childress]

"My first term here was something of a shock. Here I am right out of high school and living away from home and living in this large community. The schedule at first seemed very difficult, but was very helpful. Living with 200 plus seminarians is very interesting. It is a very positive time in history for the Church and provides tremendous support for us as seminarians. There also seems to be great fraternity in the house." [Dean Carson]

"I found my earliest days here to be very confirming. both encouraging and strengthening to me in my vocational pursuit. It was also 'new'; a semester of newness. New step, new school, new brothers, new daily attire, even a new basketball court, etc. It is encouraging to know that you are not fighting the good fight alone. To have 200+ brothers who are walking with you on this challenging journey is wonderful! It can get a little overwhelming sometimes, of course, and guys may clash here and there, but it is part of learning how to give of yourself and die to your pride many times." [J. Michael Villanueva]

"My first year in seminary was great. I adapted quickly to my new home. After all, it would be my home for the next eight years! Considering that I was not used to meeting many people that often, providentially I made friendships with people from other nationalities. We shared a common characteristic, we were somewhat considered foreigners. Even though I was born and had lived in the U.S.A. for many years, my background is Mexican. Such was the case for my closest friends. One was from Africa and the other from Asia. Others were from the west coast, and many from the south. All our experiences together made it possible for us to mingle well with each other. After all, we were all in the same boat." [Jesse Garza]

40

" My first days at the Josephinum had everything that I had been miss-ing in high school. I had friends who I could connect with on a spiritual level who are not just talking about what is on T.V. and I had a forma-tion team that cared about my whole person. I was much appreciative of the focus given to me in being formed as a man of God. There is a nice balance to living in this size of a community. You are able to know everyone on campus, but there is enough variety in the day that you can change it up with the people you interact with." **[Estevan Wetzel]**

Expectations of seminarians who enter the Josephinum:

We fully expect seminarians, at whatever level, to be appropri-ately committed life of the seminary and to contribute generously to it, and to receive substance from it.

We expect seminarians to give evidence of an ability to follow a reasonable schedule with community prayer at its heart, allowing for a healthy balance of personal prayer, study, recreation leisure and social interaction.

As a Pontifical institution, the Josephinum follows closely *The Program of Priestly Formation,* and each seminarian receives a handbook, issued with the approval of the Board of Trustees, which clearly state the expectations of the formation program of the seminary. This governing Church document of priestly development forms the basis of an annual evaluation of each seminarian at the Josephinum. It is also here that the seminarian will find the Josephinum's mission statement, policies and procedures, criteria for evaluation, calendars, schedules and other material necessary for the effective formation of future priests.

This rule of life is necessary to regulate the day to day living experiences and to articulate the common values that gives this faith community a sense of integrity and purpose. It provides a clear statement of behavioral expectations for everyone involved. It seeks to balance freedom, responsibility, accountability, activities and solitude.

Additionally, frequent Rector's conferences are conducted to help seminarians interpret rightly their life in common, the discernment of their vocations, and the human and spiritual virtues they strive to incorporate in their daily lives. Issues of celibacy and chaste living are incorporated in these Rector's conferences. They also foster development of priestly spirituality to facilitate and enhance the priest's pastoral work among the faithful.

The seminary environment itself fosters a simple way of life and a spirit of priestly detachment. Seminarians are made aware that they are responsible for the proper stewardship of materials and their own personal well-being. Appropriate respect for those in authority and mature sense of obedience are also benchmarks for seminarian development.

The Pontifical College Josephinum creates a climate for mutual respect, communication, and collaboration as a contribution to the overall development of the seminarians as they interact with other as well.

Priestly formation doesn't occur in a vacuum. Men and women mingle with seminarians in a variety of settings: personal, academic, pastoral and ecumenical. The interaction of seminarians with seminary administrative staff and service personnel often reveals attitudes toward others in general. Seminarians' ongoing contact with their own family and home community will continue to form a significant dimension of their life, and seminarians participate in parish activities and in weekly apostolic programs.

Seminarians at the Josephinum learn to appreciate the multicultural, multiethnic, and international community which is the seminary. This multifaceted environment provides a mutually enriching dimension to the seminary community and reflects the realities of pastoral life awaiting seminarians. This diversity also help seminarians to develop a quality of adaptability to varied pastoral settings in their future priestly ministry.

It's clear to even the most casual observer, that the structured life of prayer, study and reflection has a salutatory effect upon the men of the Josephinum:

"The day-to-day life can actually tax your spiritual life if you are not careful. I found that the academic rigor and demands of formation have the potential to take much away from the other facets of seminary life. We say, 'do not let your education get in the way of your formation.' Luckily our schedule of daily prayer and also the fraternity of all the brothers in the house keep this in perspective on a daily basis." **Daniel Swartz— Second Year Theology—Columbus Ohio—[Diocese of Columbus]**

>"Starting with Office of Readings and then Morning Prayer every day, I am constantly reminded of Christ as the priority of my day. It is a huge blessing to be able to have this time available for us to pray. I remember in my few years working, it is extremely difficult to make time to pray and to know how to pray. This routine at Seminary has grounded me in solid prayer habits that I can practically carry forward and build upon. Also, it reminds me how real the presence of Christ is, even during the days I experience spiritual dryness. God just wants us to show up!" **Mitchel Roman—First Year Pre-Theology—Empire MI [Diocese of Gaylord]**

"I'm very blessed to have to opportunity to attend Mass every day in-house. I enjoy praying lauds and vespers in community as well. Also, it

is very good that I have the opportunity to attend holy hour daily. Even if Our Lord is not exposed in a monstrance on the altar, I can just go to any chapel and pray or meditate in peace before his presence. It has become my custom to go before the Tabernacle and ask Our Lord for his assistance before I take a major exam. My spiritual journey has been very successful all these years. I have lived in the seminary for six years now. I have been under the authority of three very different rectors, and a few teachers who are no longer with us. Also, some of my peers who entered seminary with me have already graduated. I felt sad when some of them left; with others I felt joy because they were graduating. It has been a roller coaster of emotions with each one of them, I have become more aware of our Catholic faith, our Catholic church, and the issues which trouble our beautiful and diverse nation." [Jesse Garza]

"It reminds me that while faith and vocation are deeply personal, they are far from private. I am in seminary, not only for my own salvation and holiness, but for the salvation and holiness of my brothers, sisters, and the whole Church; and for the salvation of souls. As I did every year at Franciscan, I have become more aware of my weakness and littleness, but in turn, of all the gifts and blessings God has given me as well... all the ways in which He has led and continues to lead me in everything if I let Him." [J. Michael Villanueva]

The Continuing Evaluation of Seminarians

The Pontifical College Josephinum is responsible for the continuing evaluation of all of its seminarians. This process of evaluation is clearly defined in the student handbook and is the primary responsibility of the Rector and the faculty.

Seminarians at the Josephinum are held accountable for all aspects of priestly formation. This includes, but is not limited to, participation in spiritual exercises, the spiritual direction program, liturgical exercises, and community life as well as the academic and pastoral dimensions of priestly formation.

This approach is taken because all the aspects of priestly formation are intimately interwoven. Other inputs as appropriate may also be considered. The Josephinum also requires an evaluation of the seminarians summer activities from an appropriate supervisor. This report document the seminarian's attention to the areas of human spiritual, intellectual and pastoral formation as appropriate.

This evaluation process results in a yearly report from the rector to the diocesan Bishop sponsoring the seminarian and provides a clear estimation of the seminarians progress in all elements of formation. The annual report includes the results of a faculty vote regarding the seminarians advancement and supplies the details of how of the voting was conducted as well as its results. This evaluation process includes a well-founded judgment concerning the seminarians suitability for advancement to the next year of formation.

The Rector and the faculty consider the canonical requirements for ordination such as integral faith, right intention, requisite knowledge, good reputation, integral morals and proven virtues, and the requisite physical and psychological health. They provides sound and collective judgment as to the seminarian's aptitude for priestly life and ministry as well as an estimation of his capacity to lead a chaste, celibate life. The stage or year in which the seminarian is currently in formation is always considered in assessing his readiness for advancement.

The seminarians at the Josephinum, even if they are unaware of the higher level directives which guide the formation process are familiar with, and appreciative of, the spirit of community which is informed by these directives:

> *"I was struck by Monsignor Schreck's reflection on the three main charisms of the PCJ: Pontifical, National, and Missionary. While I've only been here a semester, my bishop was a former rector here as well as our auxiliary bishop who was a former vice rector for the college. This makes me think of their prayers and efforts which have made the PCJ and all the vocations that come through these halls possible. I love having a balance of clergy and lay professors. It helps to illustrate the universal call to holiness in the Church. I love also learning about the other cultures. It is a special blessing to hear about the many ways in which men who are from Mexico, Colombia or Myanmar have made their way to the PCJ!"* **[J. Michael Villanueva]**

> *"Monsignor Schreck delivered two memorable conferences at the beginning of the year, when he encouraged us to only worry about the things worth worrying about, and also at the beginning of this semester when he encouraged us to rediscover the joy of the Gospel that the Holy Father talked about. Every rector will have a new vision or at least a new emphasis. I have had two rectors and it has been a joy to be able to learn from two brilliant men.*

> *I have grown to appreciate the vocation of the laity and the unity of the Church as a whole. When you are not properly catechized, you can mistakenly think that holiness is only for priests. But as I've grown in seminary and witnessed the examples of the faithful back home and the faculty here, I can see the life of holiness being lived out in both men and women. It is such a consolation to see a community working together to build up the Church. The women, in particular, give a balanced and motherly love that is very much appreciated in seminary life. It is also a great opportunity to be able to interact with people from different backgrounds. It is very interesting to see the friendly arguments that*

occur among the "Yankees" and "Southerners." People also have their own idiomatic expressions at times that get lost in translation. A few times I will be talking to my Nashville friends and they use words and phrases I had never heard of before or are used in a different context in Arizona." [Estevan Wetzel]

"The Rector's conferences have always been very insightful and the conference topic has been given at the right time in the semester. It has also been a wonderful experience of having a wide variety of professors. I have had women both Catholic and non-Catholic and men both Catholic and non-Catholic. All see the importance of their service to the seminarians and the Church. Seeing them live out their faiths is very inspirational for me. It is a great learning experience of living in community. I have made friends from all over the country and the world and have learned many things from the different cultures." [Dean Carson]

"This last rector's conference was very good, in that Msgr. Schreck addressed various issues head-on; that has been the most profound I've experienced here." [Richard Childress]

"The Rector's conferences remind me of the president's addresses at college, just a little more practical since we are a small community with a very intimate religious bond. I can tell the Rector truly is tied to this institution and cares about the seminarians here. It is gratifying to know that we have a leader who we can talk to about both big and small issues and will care about them the same." [Mitchel Roman]

"When I first arrive in seminary I needed the care of a <u>father</u>. I found this in Msgr. Langsfeld who immediately took me under his wing. He even spoke Spanish to me (he wanted to practice his Spanish with me!) Two years after, I needed a <u>leader</u>, and that is what Father Wehner was to me. Even though I was scared at first, because I needed to adjust

to the new changes,I became very good friends with him. To see him transfer to another institution was hard for me. But it was the best for the institution he was sent to. He transforms places with his dynamism. Then came Msgr. Schreck, our current rector. After having needed a father and a leader, now I needed a <u>friend</u>. That is who Msgr. Schreck is to me. He is not only my rector, father and leader. He is my friend. His kindness and gentleness are right for me now.

"The hand of God is behind all of this. After all we are being formed to work in his church. I strongly believe that each one of our professors, whether they are Catholic or not, male or female, have a special role in our lives. They have always been very professional and friendly with us. Perhaps some of them are not Catholic, but they certainly act better than some other people outside of seminary who are. Perhaps that is what being catholic (with a 'small c') really means, being universal. It would be boring if all of us were of the same place or nationality. Hearing and seeing each others' stories and backgrounds is a unique experience. Although we are all different and unique, we all share the same love for God and his people. We all are together for a common reason, to discern our vocation to the priesthood." [Jesse Garza]

Seminarians at the Josephinum live the four dimensions of priestly formation. (There is a separate chapter devoted to each of these in detail later in this volume). Seminarians at the Josephinum recognize that life in community provides special graces, as well as special challenges. Each has developed his own strategies to maximize the benefits of their all-to-short time in close contact with peers who share their values and vision of the future:

"There have been conflicts, but nothing cataclysmic. It's been good to learn more and more how to negotiate them. I have a wide range of activities: reading, painting, writing poetry, working out, calling friends back home, going to a movie, or going to lunch/dinner with a

seminarian brother in my 'core' group if that is helpful in the given situation." **[Richard Childress]**

"I am used to people of differing ethnicity and culture. The house is so diverse in that regard that there is great respect for everyone's background. In fact, the comfort level is high with diversity that there is a great deal of fun made at its expense. Anyone who lives with over 200 neighbors all with very diverse backgrounds and well-formed personalities and has not found themselves in conflict is not human. This is a type of formation in itself in that it provides many opportunities to grow in patience, understanding, charity. It is a great laboratory in learning how to work with many different sorts of people in parish life. As for myself, I play soccer and water polo, take a lot of time to go hiking, hang out with fellow seminarians, or just find a good book. The summers are crucial for a seminarian to prepare for the next year and not go 'insane.' Therefore, I made a promise to myself for the summers: one adventure a year." **[Daniel Swartz]**

"There have been conflicts at times, certainly. As I said earlier, it helps us to learn how to live in community, which will always have conflicts... but conflict that is handled rightly and with humility forges stronger men and communities as 'iron sharpens iron.' To de-stress I like to run, play basketball, play guitar, hike, have a game night with close brothers, or get off campus and visit with friends." **[J. Michael Villanueva]**

"With such a small school, you are bound to get on each others nerves. But it's good for human formation. It allows you to be tested and learn how to deal with people you don't like. So this person makes you upset for whatever reason, what are you going to do? Ignore him, chew him out? No. You can't avoid the situation or get angry. You must learn the skills to approach another brother in a fraternal way and relay any problems or learn to appreciate this brother by thanking God for the

gifts he has that may not annoy you. Prayer is always key in the semi-nary! It's that simple, but not that easy. If you lose yourself and your relationship with God, you will turn into a crab. From that identity as a loved son of the Father flows the love you can give to others.

In addition, you always need that close group of friends with whom you can vent or discuss concerns. We can't live this life solitary. We are relational beings and those core friendships are crucial. There is no lone wolfing in the Diocesan priesthood!" **[Estevan Wetzel]**

"This year we are a 200-headed monster! We all have different cus-toms, experiences, etc. Still, we have to find common ground to make our experience in seminary pleasant. Nonetheless, there have been situations when I have had conflicts with my peers. Still, I keep walk-ing ahead. I'm glad God is calling me to be a priest, and not a seminar-ian! We cannot have the resurrection without the passion first. We are all different and share different perspectives about different experiences in life. But we must come together to find common ground. We swim or drown. So it is necessary to live the experience, get all the best of it, learn from it, and move on. Thanks be to God for his mercy! **[Jesse Garza]**

To live alone, isolated, in a place of community is suicide. As human beings were are all called to live in communion. After all, if I want to be a priest I have to be a man of communion. Otherwise, I'm in the wrong place! So I rely on my friends. I have classmates and peers, but above all I have friends. At the end of the day I know I can retire to my place and talk to somebody about a particular situation, a problem, or to share a joy with them. Also, I enjoy walking outside, especially in the woods. Going to the creek or at least to the lake is a nice way for me to relax or to meditate. Also, going out to the movies, to eat, or simply visit a store is necessary. There is a world outside these four walls. One must not forget that either." **[Estevan Wetzel]**

Just as with any edifice, development of a Christ-like priestly character depends on the integral strength of each of these dimensions. While the seminarian might rightly focus on different aspects of his development at different stages of his sojourn at the Josephinum, he would do well to consider the word of Jesus, as recounted in 1 Corinthians: *"Now the body is not a single part, but many. If a foot should say, because I am not a hand I do not belong to the body, it does not for this reason belong any less to the body. Or if an ear should say, because I am not an eye I do not belong to the body, it does not for this reason belong any less to the body. If the whole body were an eye, where would the hearing be? If the whole body were hearing, where would the sense of smell be? But as it is, God placed the parts, each one of them, in the body as he intended."* We will consider each of these characteristics in turn in the following chapters.

GALLERY ONE:

Potential Seminarians visit the Pontifical College Josephinum for our semi-annual live-in weekend, Spring 2012.
[Photo credit: Carolyn Dinovo – PCJ]

New seminarians are welcomed by Father Paul Hrezo at the Josephinum's orientation in 2010.
[Photo credit: Carolyn Dinovo– PCJ]

The Rector/President, Msgr Christopher Schreck presents the Annual St. Joseph Award for exceptional service to Dr. Alma Amell, Director of Hispanic Formation and Dr. David J. De Leonardis, Academic Dean and Director of College Academic Formation in March 2013,
[Photo credit: Carolyn Dinovo/Josh Altonji – PCJ]

Historical marker, placed by the state of Ohio in 2002, commemorating Msgr. Jessing, the Josepinum's founder. The plaque faces U.S. Route 23, passed by over 15,000 vehicles daily.

[Photo credit: Carolyn Dinovo/Josh Altonji – PCJ]

Seminarians Christopher Hamilton, Nathaniel Gorman, and Jonathan Eichold, at the annual Veterans' Day Commemoration, 2013.
[Photo credit: Carolyn Dinovo/Josh Altonji – PCJ]

Seminarians Avery Daniel, Jonathan Howell, Rhodes Bolster at the newly updated Bowling Alley in the restored Athletic Building.

[Photo credit: Josh Altonji – PCJ]

Seminarians Jedidiah Tritle, Andrew Ward, Joe Finke, John Bauman of the victorious "College of Cardinals" in the annual Mudbowl in 2013.

[Photo credit: Carolyn Dinovo/Josh Altonji – PCJ]

Seminarians Deacon Jose DeLeon, Evan Barraza, and Matthew Arterbery in the hard fought Mudbowl of 2013. The term "flag football" underestimates the vigor of this annual tradition.

[Photo credit: Carolyn Dinovo/Josh Altonji – PCJ]

4 ON BECOMING MORE AUTHENTICALLY HUMAN

"Since I arrived here I've learned that Jesus works through the formators and wants every human person to pursue faithfully and joyfully his call to greatness!" **Craig Osburn—Second Year Pre-Theology—Carol Stream. Il—[Diocese of Joliet]**

"My experiences here have been nothing but positive. The formation team really does seem to want you to succeed." **Gordon Mott—First Year Pre-Theology—Columbus Ohio—[Diocese of Columbus]**

As all Josephinum seminarians learn during their first days of orientation, the basic principles of human formation can be found in Pope John II's encyclical *Pastores Dabo Vobis, (I Will Give You Shepherds),* which proclaims that the human personality of the priest must be a bridge and not an obstacle for others in their meeting with Jesus Christ. Human formation, then, for seminarians at the Josephinum strives to prepare men to be effective instrument of Christ's grace. At the Josephinum, seminarians are assisted in this task by:

Formation Directors: Most frequently, these specially selected priests offer the seminarians encouragement, support and challenges in the intense environment which is a modern Catholic seminary.

They function as formators in the external forum. They constantly journey with the seminarians and assist them to grow by offering frequent feedback about their general demeanor, their relations with others, their maturity and their capacity to assume the role of a public person and community leader, and their appreciation of those the human virtues which make them suitable for the priesthood. These formators provide counsel in a variety of forms. But these formators function exclusively in the *external* forum and do not engage in matters that are reserved to the internal forum. That task is reserved for the seminarian's spiritual director.

Spiritual Directors: At the Josephinum, these specially selected priests who function in the *internal* forum, also play a significant and critical role in the spiritual formation of seminarians. When they engage in the dialogue of spiritual direction with seminarians, they are of great assistance in cultivating the virtues of self-reflection and self-discipline that are foundational for human development.

Psychological Counseling: On occasion, consultation with a psychologist can be a useful instrument of human formation, and the Pontifical College Josephinum offers seminarians appropriate access to licensed psychologists and other mental health providers. Some patterns of behavior, for example, which may have become set in the candidate's early family history, may impede his relational abilities. Understanding one's psychological history and developing strategies to address elements of negative impact can be very critical to effective human formation. In recent years a permanent deacon of the diocese of Columbus has served both as an adjunct faculty member and as the resident licensed psychologist and counselor for seminarians.

The influence of the complete formation team is deeply felt by every seminarian here:

"The formators all have their own characteristics, which is very good. They each bring something different to the Josephinum as a whole. They provide a great example to what we have to look forward to as well as setting an example of what a priest should do through their actions." **Zach Brown—Third Year College—Attica, Ohio—[Diocese of Toledo]**

"They are excellent! When I first arrived at the Josephinum, I was assigned to Dr. Cahall for formation advice. It was a special situation because my formation adviser was younger than me! Then I was assigned to Dr. Clabeaux. For the next three-and-a-half years he was my formation adviser and friend. Now my current formation adviser is Msgr. Morris who has also become a good friend and counselor. Besides them, I have also enjoyed the honor of having some wonderful spiritual directors as well. Msgr. Cleves was the man who helped me adapt to the seminary. I was very hard on myself, and he taught me to appreciate myself for who I was. Father Ciccone has been my spiritual adviser for the past three years. He makes me feel loved by God, and makes me awake and see and live reality." **Jesse Garza—Third Year Theology—Mission, TX—[Diocese of Brownsville]**

"They've been just what I needed! They have been very welcoming and genuinely care how we are doing. It is clear that their priority is to walk with us as we strive to grow into saints; holy, prayerful, and unshakable priests founded on Christ." **J. Michael Villanueva—First Year Theology—Anthem, AZ—[Diocese of Phoenix]**

Because the Josephinum has college, Pre-Theology, and theology programs, it is not unusual that the norms and expectations of human behavior will vary according to the age and experiences of the individual seminarians. It is logical and not unusual to expect different levels of development in each of these programs. At the Josephinum, faculty and administration, through their training and experience can usually determine age-appropriate behaviors for the seminarians placed in our care.

It is important to note that this type of counseling and consultation differs from extensive psychotherapy, which from time to time may be warranted if a seminarian needs to address deeply entrenched personal issues which impede their formation for the priesthood. The Josephinum has consulting relationships with other experienced clinicians, who after working with the seminarian may make a recommendation that the individual withdraw temporarily from the program and that his circumstances be seriously addressed before readmission to the program would be considered.

The priests of the Josephinum strives to integrate human formation with the other three dimensions of formation: spiritual, intellectual, and pastoral. Human formation is linked to spiritual formation by the reality that grace builds on nature and perfects nature. Human formation is linked to intellectual formation by the cultivation of the human functions of perception, analysis, and judgment.

Human formation also contributes to intellectual formation by enabling seminarians to pursue theology as a response to the questions of the human condition. Human formation is finally linked to pastoral formation, which enables a priest to connect with and care for others with his human personality. Conversely, pastoral formation sharpens his human skills and empathic capacities. We'll discuss these dimensions of formation in more detail in subsequent chapters. But, in sum, a man preparing for ordination is expected to be:

His Own Person: He must be a man who is free to fulfill his role in God's design, yet he must be one who does not —contrary to popular American culture— pursue his freedom as just the expansion of behavioral options or in detachment from others. One way that this maturity is made manifest is by examining how a seminarian spends his limited free time at the Josephinum:

"I enjoy reading. If I have my class reading done I will pick up a good book and enjoy it. I especially like Fantasy (Tolkien and Lewis) and science fiction. If I am not reading, occasionally I will catch up on a TV series that I enjoy." **[Joseph Finke]**

"I enjoy the rain very much. In fact, that is one of the reasons I love Columbus. On any given summer evening, it just starts pouring. The rainy weather her is very different from south Texas. Usually, back home, when it rains it is because a hurricane is approaching, or we end up with flash floods. Here in Columbus the rain is calming. So whenever I can, I grab my umbrella and go out to enjoy the rain. If it is too cold, then perhaps I just watch it from a window. I enjoy watching movies or reading a book on a rainy day, if I cannot go outside. I don't find much entertainment browsing the net, though." **[Jesse Garza]**

"Well if it is during school time, first is catching up on homework and reading because by far that is the most important. If all homework is done than maybe I will go watch a movie in the TV room, or go online on my computer for shows that I watch that are coming out with new episodes. Or even play a board game every once in a while." **[Zach Brown]**

"Movie nights! I like to play the indoor games, like ping pong, foosball, and shooting pool. I also enjoy playing Dominion; a unique and very fun card, battle, and strategy game." **[Craig Osburn]**

"I'm usually in the gym but if its late I'll socialize in the pub, play ping-pong pool or watch sports. I occasionally surf You Tube." **[Blaise Radel]**

Josephinum seminarians have a wide variety of options to ensure that they have both the physical and mental strength to serve the faithful:

"I particularly enjoy working out in the cardio room and playing basketball, on intramural as well as the competitive travel and tournament team. Also, I enjoy taking walks around the beautiful campus, especially Lake George* and the ravine behind it, as well as playing guitar, especially outside when it is warm under a tree or near the Lake. **[J. Michael Villanueva]**

"I enjoy walking very much. I like to pray the rosary as I walk to the lake and around the property. It is very peaceful and soothing. Also, every now and then I go to the St. Joseph or St. Rose of Lima chapels at night to spend some quiet time with our Lord. That helps very much." **[Jesse Garza]**

"I like to play softball in the fall and spring. nothing beats being outside on a nice day playing some softball with a great group of guys. I also played soccer my first year but not so much anymore." **[Zach Brown]**

"It is hardly an overstatement to say that I love Sunday afternoon softball games. There is nothing better than praising the Lord all

morning long in Mass and adoration, and then praising the Lord with our bodies by using them to play softball. The games are always great chance to grow in virtue and fraternity, and to really get to know your brother seminarians in a more personal, down to earth way." **[Joseph Finke]**

"I like intramural basketball, tennis, ping pong, swimming, jogging, billiards, etc. I like to stay in shape and be fit, and there is a wide variety of ways to be fit and have fun doing it!" **[Craig Osburn]**

"For me, the pub and sports are the greatest stress reducers here. The pub is a great source of fraternal support in the evening. I also enjoy the vibrant and active athletic community here that is always setting up games and matches in various sports." **Joseph Dalheim— Second Year Theology—Temple, TX [Diocese of Austin]**

A seminarian should also strive to be:

A Good Communicator: At the Josephinum, seminarians learn to be effective listeners, and develop skills of effective communication particularly as it applies to public speaking.

A Person of Emotional Maturity: Seminarians at the Pontifical College Josephinum are assisted in becoming men whose feelings are in balance and integrated throughout their thoughts and values. We strive to assist them in becoming men of feelings who are not driven by these feelings, but freely live their lives enriched by them. This is especially manifested by their willing ability to live comfortably with authority and to take necessary direction, yet also prepared to exercise authority maturely amongst peers and to deal effectively with conflict and stress.

In this context, one of the longest standing traditions at the Josephinum is the annual "Mud Bowl" pitting the Collegians against the Theologians in a very spirited game of flag football. Don't let the name fool you – this late autumn game can get rough and tumble! Over the years, it's become the centerpiece for many traditions, and priest-alumni have been known to travel hundreds of miles to attend the big game, and to participate in the various celebrations which complete the weekend. Suffice it to say, the busiest and most valuable player on the field is often the school nurse!

"I actually had the wonderful privilege to be the 'Mud Bowl Pope' for this year's Mud Bowl. This tradition consists of the College Hall Prefects and President of the Seminarian Council coming together and choosing someone to lead the College team as mascot. The College team is the "College of Cardinals" while Theology are the 'Papal Bulls'. Vinhson, the president, fooled me into thinking I was going to the front office for errands and as we entered the board room, the lights turned on and everyone was assembled in conclave. They announced their decision and I had to come up with a name! I chose Juan Diego because Our Lady of Guadalupe is the patroness of the Americas.

This was providential because it turns out that we had lost the old design for the Mud Bowl Tee shirts and we decided to put Our Lady of Guadalupe on the back of the shirt. In addition, we decided to dedicate the whole team to Our Lady of Guadalupe. It was quite a lot of fun. The night before the game, I gave a speech from the second floor and presented an image of Our Lady Of Guadalupe from the window.

Then all of the college moves to the field for a bonfire. Traditionally the Pope gets to ride in a pope mobile (this year it was Max's mustang). But I chose to have Mary in the vehicle instead. We had guys wearing ponchos and cassocks. Then there was smores! We honored Mary the next day as well with a procession. And what as a result? The College won! I have to say that Our Lady was helping us out since we honored her. We had the image on the sidelines the whole game. It was really awesome to turn a fun tradition into something spiritual and dedicate the game to Mary." **Estevan Wetzel—Fourth Year College— Phoenix, AZ.—[Diocese of Phoenix]**

"I have participated in the Mud Bowl for four years. The first two years I played in the Mud Bowl and my last two years of the college I coached the Mud Bowl. I enjoyed both experiences. It is a big game. In my mind it is similar to the Ohio State— Michigan Game." **[Dean Carson]**

"I've played in four Mud Bowls; we've won three of those times. Winning is great, but the year we lost. the College put together a great team and the better team won for sure! The most fun I've had playing was when everyone is relaxed and we're just having a good time. That was most evident for me in the fall of 2012 when I was in Second Theology. We were just having fun. We won that year too, which was even better." **[Michael Hartge]**

"I have never played in the Mud bowl, but I have assisted in taking pictures for several events. Perhaps one of the most memorable events was when Father Mengele played. He was so physical that he even got hurt. I took the picture that immortalized the man, blood and all." **[Jesse Garza]**

Additionally, the seminarian is expected to be:

A Collaborator: He must also be a man who relates well with others and is willing to work with people of diverse backgrounds. He must strive to be a man capable of wholesome relationships with men and women as relatives, friends, colleagues, members of the staff and faculty as well as anyone encountered during his apostolic work.

A Faithful Steward: At the Josephinum seminarians learn to be good stewards of material possessions: someone who is able to live a simple life and be able to avoid whatever has a semblance of vanity. He maintains a correct attitude toward the temporal needs of the church, and possesses a mature attitude toward worldly possessions. He is expected to be a man who is generous in making charitable contributions and in sustaining and affirming the poor and underprivileged. It is not a coincidence that Pope Francis has recently spoken forcefully about clergy who have confused their private comforts and status with the will of God, and the needs of the faithful.

A Public Man: The seminarian must become a man who can take on the role of a public person: someone both secure in himself and convinced of his responsibility. He is able to live not just as a private citizen, but as a public person in service of the Gospel who represents the Church.

On this topic, the semi-isolated seminarians of Monsignor Jessing's day and seminarians today would find that their situations differed greatly. Most have automobiles and have plenty of opportunity to get away for a while:

"I'd say that I frequently go off campus every now and again. I'm a member of the Columbus Museum of Art, so I have that as an option, or I go help out at my parish sometimes on weekends. This week, I'm going to a poetry reading featuring one of our administrative staff, and I hope to take a few guys along." **[Gordon Mott]**

"I really don't go off campus too much because there is so much to do here! But when we do, we like seeing movies, going to the bar for a drink, getting ice cream, and yes, even Walmart can be really fun at times." **[Craig Osburn]**

"I don't go off campus that much, maybe a few times a week. We go out to eat, go to the movies, go shopping, and I also drive my group to our apostolic assignment." **[Zach Brown]**

"I enjoy going to golf courses, theaters, and different cultural centers." **[Dean Carson]**

"The Drexel movie theater in Bexley is a cool place to go see movies. It's nice to put some distance between you and the PCJ every once in a while and this place does the trick. It's fun to go there to see a movie then grab a beer or some ice cream before heading back. Graeters Ice Cream Parlor in Worthington might be kept in business solely by priests and seminarians from the Josephinum! Going to Catholic high school football games around the area in the fall is also a great way to spend a Friday night. We Columbus guys usually see people we know from the parishes. That keeps you grounded, talking to them. It reminds you that you're doing this to serve the people of your diocese. This is Jesus' priesthood after all." **[Michael Hartge]**

The signature characteristic of seminarians and priests hasn't changed, however:

Celibacy: Certainly one of the most critical functions of the Josephinum is to communicate effectively to seminarians and enable them to appropriately comprehend:

- The physical and psychological understanding of human sexuality.

- The meaning of the virtue of chastity; this includes a formation in authentic ideals of sexual maturity and chastity, including virginity;

- It also includes proper knowledge of the duties and dignity of Christian marriage which represents the love which exists between Christ and the Church.

- The requisite skills for living chastely: Ascetic practice, prudent self-mastery, and paths of self-knowledge, such as a regular personal inventory and the examination of conscience.

- The meaning of celibate chastity, especially the theological rationale that makes clear how it pertains to the logic of the ordained priesthood.

- The means to live celibate chastity well, which include genuine friendships; priestly fraternity; a mentoring relationship; spiritual direction; priestly asceticism, which honestly reckons with the sacrifices that celibacy entails; and, especially, the sacrament of Penance.

- The spiritual path that transforms the experience of loneliness into a holy solitude based on a strong, lively, and personal love for Jesus Christ.

The prospect of life-long celibacy can be very off-putting. The faculty places great emphasis on this immutable characteristic of priesthood in the Latin (Roman Catholic) tradition:

"You said it, most especially for young men. However, when one comes to know more the truth of celibate love; the unquenchable, burning, selfless, sacrificial love of Jesus Christ, celibacy becomes mysteriously irresistible to the heart that is made to be filled by it and to give it away to the whole world!" **[J. Michael Villanueva]**

72

"This is an important topic for the Church and seminary formation today. We hear about it often because we cannot ignore it. It's ultimately a gift and charism that the Lord offers to those whom he calls to the priesthood. We have had weekend workshops on the topic of celibacy. It helps you to make sure you have really thought about it and understand it. No one is forced to accept it because no one is forced to be ordained. However, when one freely chooses to be ordained and it is determined that he has a call, then he should have thought and prayed about this at length." **Michael Hartge —Third Year Theology—Reynoldsburg, OH—[Diocese of Columbus**

"Formators show that its not just a cross but a joy in the sense that its not what you now cannot do: namely have biological children, but now you can become the father to thousands of spiritual children. Its a discipline that make us more available to the people of God and I've really taken that to heart." **Blaise Radel—Second Year College— Arlington,Va—[Diocese of Arlington]**

"The priests here have been very helpful. Both personally in formation meetings and as well as having conferences on celibacy. Books have helped that have been recommended regarding the joy of living celibacy as a priest. These books have really helped in my understanding of celibacy as a good thing." **Zach Brown—Third Year College—Attica, Ohio—[Diocese of Toledo]**

"The faculty have done a good job of helping me to understand the purpose and blessing of life-long celibacy. With this understanding, I can embrace celibacy as a source of life-givings to the Church and fruitfulness for those I am intended to serve. It allows for the full com- mitment of oneself to the Church through selfless, sacrificial love that the Church might be brought ever-closer to its spouse, Christ Jesus" **[Joseph Dalheim]**

In Summary —The Tools of Human Formation:

At the Josephinum, every seminarian participates in:

- Instruction: The rector and other faculty members offer the seminarians the Church's vision of human formation through conferences, courses and other educational means.

- Personal reflection: Josephinum seminarians are trained to live life reflectively and to examine, with regularity, their behavior, their motivations, their inclinations, and, in general, their appropriation of life experience, especially suffering.

- Community life and feedback: At the Josephinum we fully expect that any seminarian who freely chooses to enter the seminary must also freely accept and respect its terms. The demands and the rewards at the Josephinum expand self-knowledge and self-control and cultivate generosity of spirit. The community's attachment to the Word of God and the sacramental life provides a reflective mirror that helps individuals know themselves and summons them to a fuller, more human, more spiritual life.

So, the critical question for young seminarians is this: how has the human formation program changed me?

"I pleaded my case before my bishop so I could continue my formation at the Josephinum after I completed my undergraduate studies. I asked him to continue my theology studies here because I liked the institution, its leadership, and its academic challenges. I strongly believe that if I had been sent to continue my studies somewhere else, after having been here for my college studies, I would have not been as happy as I am right now. I chose the best there is for my formation. I'm very grateful

to my bishop and my diocese to have allowed me to stay here. Here I had the opportunity to go see Pope Benedict XVI when he came to New York. Most recently, I served Mass for our Pope Francis on New Years Day 2014. I have had experiences here that perhaps I would not have if I had been elsewhere. To have been sent to study here at the Josephinum, and to have been allowed to stay here for my theology studies afterward, has been providential. I have been formed as a good man to serve God and our church. I'm proud to be a true product of the Josephinum!" **[Jesse Garza]**

"From day one of orientation, I feel I have grown every day into a stronger man of God. The opportunity to be intensely formed as a man has given me the opportunity to confront my deepest fears, weaknesses, etc., not alone, but with God along side me, leading me. Because of this, like gold is tried in fire, so too have I been formed and will continue to be formed in the seminary. The experience of brotherhood has strengthened me and the experience in the classroom has stoked the fire in my heart to know God more, as well as to bring to others in a radical, personal, and daily encounter with Jesus Christ." **[J. Michael Villanueva]**

"I think my time here has been well spent because so far I feel I'm in the right place. That's what gives me joy and inner peace. If I were to be ordained tomorrow I would really miss this place because of the fraternity founded in Christ through Liturgy and Sacraments as well as the organized structure of the place. And it is a beautiful campus!" **[Blaise Radel]**

"The Josephinum has changed me into a completely different person. I was quiet when I first entered; now people say they can't get me to be quiet at times. My prayer life has grown, friendships have developed into a support group where we can talk about things that are bothering us. Seminary is great; I was scared coming here my first year, and

now three years later I am the happiest I have ever been, loving life and happy that I came to the Josephinum." **[Zach Brown]**

"The Josephinum has changed me for the better for sure. I know that I am more patient and understanding in general. I know that these interactions with the seminarians and direction from our formators will all do me well as I prepare to serve the People of God as a priest one day." **[Michael Hartge]**

" Its made me a better person overall. I think I relate to people better, have a more balanced and virtuous approach to life (hopefully), and love God and His people more purely." **[Joseph Dalheim]**

The rule of life at the Josephinum has been structured to foster the seminarians' discipline, self-mastery, and faithful perseverance in their commitments. This commitment is made manifest through thorough application to the tasks of seminary life. Human formation develops through interaction with others in the course of the seminary program. This growth happens, for example, when seminarians learn to accept the authority of the formators, develop the habit of using freedom with discretion, learn to act on their own initiative and do so energetically, and learn to work harmoniously with confreres and laity.

*   * Named in honor of of Father George Kempker (1913-1971), alumnus ordained in 1939 who served with distinction as a Navy Chaplain in WW-II.*

5 SPIRITUAL FORMATION FOR PRIESTHOOD

"I have come to know the love that Jesus has for me in the Eucharist. It IS life. It's Jesus. He's the way, the truth, and the life. Without the Eucharist, the whole world would be dying from lack of love." **Craig Osburn—Second Year Pre-Theology—Carol Stream. Il—[Diocese of Joliet]**

A disinterested observer might legitimately assume that the goals of human, intellectual, and perhaps even pastoral formation, might be adequately achieved in settings other than a Roman Catholic seminary. For example, there's not much question that military boot camp can have a life changing impact on recruits as human beings (the current Marine Corps recruiting slogan *Be All You Can Be* seems to echo a lot of the concepts covered in human formation.)

Consider also that the Josephinum's well- deserved nickname *"West Point on the Olentangy"* presumes that the U.S. Military Academy on the heights overlooking the Hudson is itself no slouch when it comes to academic rigor and intellectual formation.

And ministry to the poor and distressed — the helpless, home-less and hopeless — has unquestionably profited from the selfless service of deacons, sisters, brothers and charitable laypersons, none of whom have ever set foot on seminary grounds. No, it is the deep spiritual formation of men for the priesthood, lasting for six, eight, or even more years which forms the *sine qua non* of the seminary experience.

You see, the primary call to discipleship is *conversion of heart*. The practice of spiritual formation is itself a synthesis of the teachings of the Catholic Church. One lives in intimate and unceasing union with God the Father through Jesus and the Holy Spirit. Jesus invited his apostles to come to him before he sent them out to others. St. Augustine alluded to this double identity and commitment when he said to his people *"With you I am a Christian, for you I am a bishop."*

At the Josephinum, spirituality is focused upon the Eucharistic sacrifice in the transformation of our lives by the power of the redeeming love of Jesus Christ. It is the source of pastoral charity, that love which animates and directs those who aspire to the priesthood. It is the source and the summit of our life at the Josephinum, indeed, the celebration of the Holy Eucharist is the "essential moment of our day" for every seminarian:

> *"The Eucharist has been and continues to be the driving force of my life as a seminarian. At the Josephinum, some of my fondest memories are those connected with our yearly Corpus Christi processions and the recently restored forty hours devotion. Each time we process around campus behind Our Lord in the Blessed Sacrament on Corpus Christi, I am reminded of the awesome reality that we are not called to lead, but to allow Christ to lead us - and lead others through us. Our times of Eucharistic devotion, such as the forty hours, where we are united in prayer around the Eucharist, remind me that the deepest brotherhood we have as seminarians is that which is founded on our relationship to Christ in the Eucharist!*

I have definitely experienced the Eucharist, as Sacrosanctum Concilium so eloquently puts it, as the "source and summit" of my life. I am energized to pray, study and recreate through my daily reception of Jesus in the Eucharist at Mass and am called to the heights through praying before the Eucharist at our daily holy hours." **Tom Gardner—Third Year Theology—Bexley, OH—[Diocese of Columbus]**

"It is absolutely essential! While I've always gone to Sunday Mass this acknowledgment that the Eucharist is the center of my life has not always been the case. This grew over the years especially after college and before entering seminary. I went to daily Mass one day a week when it was in the evening partly because I was thinking about the priesthood, but also because I lived in a small town at the time, didn't know anyone and thought it would be a good way to spend 45 minutes in the evening. I know now that was the beginning of a deepening of my love for the Mass and the Eucharist. It has grown exponentially since being in the seminary. Daily Mass is essential with Eucharistic adoration just as much so. Even in your driest moments, when in front of the Blessed Sacrament you at least know you're not alone. You know it. In these moments you know it's okay not to be praying for anything specific. I'm content to just spend time in the presence of the tabernacle because I'm spending time with a person, Jesus Christ. And he's alive." **Michael Hartge —Third Year Theology—Reynoldsburg, OH—[Diocese of Columbus]**

"The Eucharist, to borrow the saying from the Church, is the source and summit of my life! Studying to be a priest, the Eucharist will be the most important reality in our lives, and so we come to know and encounter Christ in that sacrament here in seminary. Whether the day is going well or poorly, it is the Eucharist that we can turn to, hand over our blessings and challenges to our Lord, and receive from Him the graces needed to carry out His work". **Joshua**

Bartlett— Third Year Theology—Liberty. MO—[Diocese of KC/ St. Joseph]

"The Eucharist is the supreme symbol of the sacramental reality of our oneness with Christ. At each Mass, we become His in the most perfect way through the beauty of the sacrament of the Eucharist. The Eucharist was where the seed for my vocation was planted (by altar serving at a young age) and it continues to sustain and enrich my life in the Lord." **Joseph Dalheim— Second Year Theology—Temple, TX [Diocese of Austin]**

"As the Catechism says, the Eucharist is the source and summit of the Christian life. For me, the Eucharist is the heart of my day and what I look forward to most. By having Mass in the morning, we are nourished for the day and take on whatever the Lord gives us each day. I am replenished when I pray a holy hour or just spend a few moments in the chapel throughout the day." **Estevan Wetzel—Fourth Year College—Phoenix, AZ.—[Diocese of Phoenix]**

Likewise the frequent participation in the Sacrament of Penance fosters the mature recognition of our sinfulness, facilitates continuous conversion of heart and spirit, and fosters growth of virtue and conformity to the mind of Christ. It is the school of compassion which instructs the seminarian how to live with compassionate mercy in the world. This frequent celebration of penance is assisted by the practice of daily ongoing examination of conscience.

While these sacraments are the capstones of our spiritual formation, they are much facilitated by participation in:

The Liturgy of the Hours: Through the liturgy of the hours we at the Josephinum learn to pray *with* the Church and *for* the Church.

Seminarians unite themselves with the body of Christ and unceasing praise and petition. These prayers prepare the seminarians for their lifelong ministry as priests who pray unceasingly on behalf of the whole Church. The Liturgy of the Hours also cultivate a mind and heart attuned to the whole body of Christ, its needs, its sufferings, and its hopes.

> *"Liturgy of the Hours has come to play an influential role in the way I go about my day. You have to keep in mind when you will be able to pray each hour of the breviary during the day. It is a challenge but it allows us to pray for the Church as a whole everyday."* **Zach Brown—Third Year College—Attica, Ohio—[Diocese of Toledo]**

> *"Like breathing. Each hour of prayer is like breathing in; a moment of rest in which we take in what is essential for life. Going forth from prayer is like breathing out; where what we breath in transforms us and moves us forward and outward towards others and the world, eventually leading us back to God."* **J. Michael Villanueva—First Year Theology—Anthem, AZ—[Diocese of Phoenix]**

> *"The Liturgy of the Hours helps to continually center my heart on the Lord throughout the day. It is so easily to become distracted and disturbed with the countless concerns of the world. The Liturgy of the Hours presents me with the opportunity to stop and renew my commitment to being in the Lord's presence and to renew my gratitude for His continued blessings that He showers upon me throughout the day."* **[Joseph Dalheim]**

> *"Throughout my time at seminary, I have grown immensely in my love and appreciation of the Liturgy of the Hours. I have come to understand more and more the Church's wisdom in requiring this daily rhythm of prayer. Our life is naturally dominated by many routines and*

rhythms - sleep and wakefulness, meals, work and recreation, talking and silence. Thus, it has been a great experience of grace building on nature to incorporate the Church's daily rhythm of prayer into my life. I more and more have found that the Liturgy of the hours allows me to "pray at all times," as St. Paul suggests, by allowing prayer to be part of each different moment in my daily routine." [Tom Gardner]

"When I first came to seminary seven years ago, I was not used to praying the Liturgy of the Hours. It was a very different form of prayer than what I was used to and took me a while to learn how to pray. Now, the Liturgy of the Hours is not only something that helps to sustain me through the day, but also is a beautiful way of staying connected to our Lord, even on those days where it can be difficult to meditate. Often I do not have the "correct" words to pray, but in the Liturgy of the Hours the Lord gives me the words that I need through His Holy Scripture." [Joshua Bartlett]

"This is more and more an extension of the Mass and an ideal place in which to lift prayer intentions that I receive from time to time. I keep pictures, prayer cards, and prayer lists in my breviary to help me to remember to pray for those who have asked for it, even those who haven't asked for it, and those who are praying for me." [Michael Hartge]

Spiritual Direction: As described in the previous chapter, the Josephinum requires that each seminarian meet regularly with an approved spiritual director. This director assists in the internalization and integration which is needed for a growth in sanctity, virtue, and readiness for holy orders.

Personal Meditation: The habit of daily prayer and meditation enables the seminarian to develop a personal understanding of how God's salvation has acted in their lives and how they might better respond to that great gift. The custom of silence is faithfully observed at the Pontifical College Josephinum, since it is during these times that seminarians learn to be attuned to God's movement in their lives. It fosters development of a contemplative attitude that finds God in all things. It gradually matures in such a manner as to allow for a balanced and unified rhythm of life in both action and contemplation, labor and prayer, and provides the future priest with the strength, meaning and focus needed in pastoral life.

Sacred Scripture: All seminarians at the Pontifical College Josephinum are encouraged and directed to develop the habit of daily reflection on the Sacred Scripture, both by daily meditation on the Lectionary readings and by other reflective readings of Sacred Scripture:

"Especially after receiving the ministry of Lector, the Sacred Scriptures have become a daily encounter with God in my life. Lectio Divina has become a true source of strength for me as I set aside time daily for prayer and reflection. I look forward to that quiet time I have in the morning with my Lord, both in the Tabernacle and in the Sacred Text." **[Joshua Bartlett]**

"I have grown in my love for Sacred Scripture at the Josephinum. By coming into more contact with the Word both through increased study and prayer, I have been able to more clearly listen to God speaking every day in the Scriptures. Through studying the Scriptures, my appreciation of God's power and wisdom has grown by seeing how He works and communicates through the human authors of the Scriptures in so many ways". **[Tom Gardner]**

"Scripture is so life- giving. I have more of a desire to try to memorize passages and to gain a better understanding of it. It is not simply an academic pursuit, although this is part of what we do here. To read it and pray with it is to get to know a person, Jesus Christ. To see how

*the Old Testament allegorically points to him, and how he gives us
an example by which to live in the New Testament. I want to know
Scripture in order to better apply it to the lives of the people I will one
day serve. I want to know it to be able to give them a good, uplifting
word when they need it most. Knowing it will help me be a better instrument of the Lord."* **[Michael Hartge]**

*"Sacred Scripture is the portal through which I encounter Christ in a
very tangible way. My daily personal prayer usually involves the reflection and meditation upon the Sacred Scriptures. Through this, the
reality of the personhood of Christ becomes ever-more alive in my heart.
My relationship with Him is able to grow through the reading of His
life and teaching and I become strengthened for the day and reminded of
my true identity as His son."* **[Joseph Dalheim]**

*"We have some great homilists here at seminary and I often find the
Scriptures opened to me when I hear them preach. Their example and
wisdom inspire me to continue to delve into the Scripture and a tangible
way I have done this by reading the Gospel of the day the night before
and again before Mass. It is a great blessing to wake up and go to sleep
with the words of the Lord on your mind."* **[Estevan Wetzel]**

Willing Obedience: At the Josephinum, seminarians learn to
surrender one's own will for the sake of a larger mission. In this
way candidates for the priesthood develop a growing and deep solidarity within the church and with their fellow laborers in the vine-
yard. This spiritual formation in chastity and celibacy are elements
of this willing obedience, not to individuals, but to the Church and
its Magisterium.

Simplicity of Life: Although not a monastic institution, life at
the Josephinum encourages a simple approach to the material goods

of the world. Seminarians are thus freed from excessive concern about possessions, and learn to exercise responsible stewardship over material things by using them in a manner which is both receptive to God's call and ecologically responsible. This is particularly important in light of American affluence in relation to other parts of the world.

Retreats and Days of Recollection: The Josephinum schedules regular periods of more intense prayer throughout the school year, which are eagerly awaited and greatly appreciated by everyone involved:

"The silent retreat is always one of the best weeks of the year. They are peaceful and refreshing. We did our deacon canonical retreat in Assisi this year. Five days in that beautiful, historic, holy city was even better than I could have anticipated. Our retreat master used the account of Our Lord's journey to Jericho from Luke 18. Just as he asked the Blind Man what he wanted him to do for him, he asks us the same thing. We too must ask that of the people we will serve." **[Michael Hartge]**

"The world is a noisy and chaotic place while God is quiet and peaceful. It can be hard going though the daily routine, sometimes finding God in prayer and sometimes not being able to quiet myself enough to recognize His presence. It is always a great joy and blessing to be given a day of recollection to once again refocus myself and find God in my life. Nothing in life is better than a day, or even better five days of silence to give me that chance to just be with God!" **[Joshua Bartlett]**

"Our yearly week-long silent retreats have been especially fruitful in introducing me to the "school of silence." Having such a long time to be unplugged from all the noisiness of life has attuned me more to the quiet

ways which God speaks in my day to day life. Growing in my ability to be silent with God has helped me to more easily discern His leading and follow it." [Tom Gardner]

"Like the Liturgy of the Hours, retreats present a more extended opportunity to be reminded of my vocation and the roots of my calling. They allow for the silence and stillness of mind that is needed to be renewed in love and the opportunity for the Lord to speak more clearly in my heart (allowing greater clarity for further spiritual purification)." [Joseph Dalheim]

"They are very helpful and allow time to get away from classes and refocus on a time of prayer. It allows time for closer reflection and meditation and more time to pray. The silent retreat is also very interesting. The first year is hard especially since we live in such a noisy world. But the silence allows you to be constantly in prayer which is a great thing." [Zach Brown]

Pious Devotion: The pious traditions of the Catholic Church, including Eucharistic Adoration, are observed regularly at the Josephinum. Devotional prayer including the Holy Rosary are observed both in public and private settings by Josephinum seminarians. Our seminarians learn to sustain their sense of community through communal devotion which also assists them in understanding the rich cultural diversity of American life.

"Firstly, it is such a privilege to have four chapels on campus in which we can adore our Lord in the Eucharist at any time. This really helps to make the seminary a true house of prayer. But beyond this, we are able to have a Holy Hour six times a week in the context of exposition - which is awesome. Being able to pray in front of Jesus exposed in the Blessed Sacrament almost every day that I have been in seminary has been the driving force of my vocation. It gives me a daily space in which

I can 'look Jesus in the eye' and have Him look at me. This mutual gaze has helped me to understand more deeply who I am in Jesus as a beloved adopted son of the Father. In addition, my devotion to Mary and the saints has definitely deepened at the Josephinum. One way this has happened is through the experience of praying with the sacred art that is everywhere on campus. Through admiring and praying with some of the beautiful statues and stain glass windows, especially in St. Joseph Oratory, I have more and more realized the beauty of the Saints and their witness to Christ. This has urged me on in my own devotion, calling me to the holiness which made them beautiful. Finally, praying through song is an important part of my devotional life. Whether it be through Praise and Worship, singing at Mass or through chanting the Liturgy of the Hours, I find much fruit from being able to sing praises to God. Music has consistently allowed me to express my deepest hopes, fears and joys to God." **[Tom Gardner]**

"I always find that when I am faithful to my daily Holy Hour (especially when in the presence of the Holy Eucharist), my day is a blessing and a joy. It doesn't matter if I experience extremely trying events during the day; if I have had time with the Lord, He is able to reveal to me His will and presence throughout those daily events, no matter how trying or frustrating. I also find that my relationship with Mary has strengthened. Now, I count her as a daily companion in learning to love more purely and perfectly. Her fiat is the guiding light for all that I attempt to do during the day. She has taught me the humble faithfulness and trust that is so necessary for growth in the spiritual life. I also believe that The Examen prayer of St. Ignatius of Loyola has helped me continually be mindful of the Lord's activity in my life each day and in each moment." **[Joseph Dalheim]**

Reconciliation: Life in the community fosters the spirit of reconciliation amongst the seminarians at the Josephinum. A non-violent way of life and a sense of peacekeeping and peacemaking is fostered amongst everyone at the Josephinum, be it priest, seminarian or laity.

Solidarity: The papal exhortation *Ecclesia in America* identified the critical importance of the path of solidarity for the Church in the American hemisphere. It is expressed in Christian love which seeks the good of others, especially of those most in need. At the Josephinum, the spiritual formation of seminarians leads them to solidarity with others, especially those most in need, through a commitment to justice and peace and more authentic missionary spirit to serve those downtrodden, where and when the need is greatest.

Solitude: We are never so close to God as when we are alone. It is then that the "still small voice"of the Creator can be heard. Part of the spiritual journey for Josephinum seminarians is developing an understanding of the differences between just being alone, or lonely, and being in a holy solitude with our Creator. The goal of the Josephinum is to assist in the establishment of these attitudes, habits and practices which will continue after ordination. Consider:

"Being a very outgoing person, it took me a long time to get used to solitude. It was only after I developed a true relationship with our Lord that solitude made sense. It is not a time to be alone and self centered, but a time to be set apart from everyone else and encounter God, even while doing normal things like laundry and cleaning my room. I now long for that solitude often. Not only do I encounter God more in those moments, but they also help to teach me how to make the other work I do a true offering to God." [Joshua Bartlett]

"Solitude plays the role in my spiritual life of reminding me that my relationship with God is the most important relationship in my life. By being able to be alone with Him, I have more and more discovered His love for me personally. And this personal experience of His love has

in turn driven me to try to share this love more and more with others."
[Tom Gardner]

"Being alone is running away from others. Being in solitude is running to the Lord to be only with Him. In this sense, times of solitude are ESSENTIAL for the spiritual life." **[J. Michael Villanueva]**

"Solitude is extremely necessary for a healthy spiritual life, for God needs intimate time alone with me, just as I need time alone with one of my parents or siblings. You cannot have the same deep conversations when you are in a group of people compared to when you are one on one. I am an extravert and enjoy being a part of a social scene constantly, so solitude is very difficult. But as I have been more intentional on praying and reading in solitude each day, designating more and more time to it, I have become more peaceful and see the amazing fruits from it." **Mitchel Roman—First Year Pre-Theology—Empire MI [Diocese of Gaylord]**

"Formation teaches you to be comfortable with your self and grow as an independent man. It's not that you don't need others, because you do, but we develop the skills and prayer habits necessary to be comfortable in our own skin and be able to spend time alone with the Lord. Solitude is a key practice to cultivate, especially during retreats, because the priestly life is an intimate and exclusive relationship with the Lord. It is from that relationship you have with the Lord that flows the love you have for your parish." **[Estevan Wetzel]**

Upon establishment as a Pontifical Seminary, the Josephinum was placed under the authority of the Congregation for the Propagation of the Faith, and later the Congregation for Catholic Education. From 1893 until the mid-1970s, Josephinum seminarians wore a cassock identical to those at the Collegium Urbanum, the congregation's seminary for overseas students atop Rome's Janiculum Hill.

The Josephinum, after prayerful reflection, discontinued use of the cassock for reasons related to the ecclesiastic climate following Vatican II and a renewed emphasis on the Church in the United States. Even so, it was clear that the change was made in reflection of the needs of the day; the decision was strategic, but never intended to be perpetual.

The cassock was re-introduced in 2011. There seems to be some differences in opinion about this recent change. For the collegians, and other junior seminarians, the change was welcomed:

Pontifical cassocks were one of the biggest enticements for me to want my bishop to send me here I thought they were SO COOL! Something out of a movie!" **[Blaise Radel]**

"I think it is not used enough. I like the idea of bringing it back, since at one time all pontifical seminaries had their own cassock and it was a way of distinguishing themselves from other seminaries. Currently we only wear it on Sundays and Holy Days of Obligation, but I would like to see it worn on all major feasts and then wear it throughout the day, rather than just for Liturgies. (for that matter I would like to see it become our uniform day in and day out, but that might be a little optimistic.) Joseph Finke—Third Year College—Ft.Wright, Ky.— [Diocese of Covington]

"They are fine. It is nice to wear them and show our pontifical status but sometimes it doesn't make sense. They are not the most comfortable things but we have to wear them quite often it seems, not so much now as my first year here. I guess I am in the boat that is neutral in this regard." **[Zach Brown]**

This sentiment is by no means universal. The older, more mature seminarians express some reservations regarding this change:

"Great, as long as it does not become a focus of vanity or superiority. Distinctions like that are an honor and should be held as such. It gives guys a good pride in being a special part of the Universal Church." [J. Michael Villanueva]

"It was well intentioned for sure. However in hind sight maybe not the best idea to do so. I think it was reintroduced to give us a visible sign of our unique identity as a seminary with pontifical status. However, it didn't seem to be too well received by many priests in some of our dioceses. It was just seen as suspicious and unnecessary by a lot of them. So while they are unique, I could have done without it because of how their reimplementation was interpreted and received by many priest alumni." [Michael Hartge]

"I think it is a good idea for Sunday liturgies here. However, I think this is only possible and appropriate because of the relatively closed and private nature of our seminary. If we were more open to the public or had more visitors, I would prefer we didn't wear the pontifical cassock. The reason is that I think it could come off as arrogant. [Joseph Dalheim]

As the Rector who re-instated the practice wrote at the time: "We are, indeed, a Roman Seminary, in and for the Americas. The Josephinum possesses a unique, historical relationship with the Holy See. The formation program unifies both the national and universal aspects of modern evangelization. Integrated into the priestly formation program is the thought of the Supreme Pontiff himself. The relationship that seminarians have with the Holy Father takes on a very personal meaning which will enrich their priestly ministry when they return to their home dioceses after ordination."

The Church is sacramental by her very nature. Using the signs and symbols given to us, we express our faith in a public way.

Re-institution of the pontifical cassock in 2011 was but a small way for seminarians to express their unique relationship to the Church; the history they belong to at the Josephinum; and how to maturely express in a proper way the meaning of clerical attire. Developing a deep spiritual life and appreciation for the mystery of our faith also requires witness. Yet Seminarians cannot hide behind the externals nor misuse the meaning of those symbols.

The use of the pontifical cassock recognizes years of spiritual maturation, appropriate use of externals, and deepened awareness of how to present oneself professionally. It is not a throw back to the past, nor an attempt to reclaim a false identity, nor a way to create barriers between priest and the laity. Rather, it reemphasizes to the future priest the distinctive character of priesthood with his unique formation at the Josephinum.

At the present time, college seminarians/pre-theologians continue to wear a shirt and tie; while theologians continue to wear simple clerical attire in class. Outside of class time, the seminarians continue to dress casually.

Seminarians wear the pontifical cassock for Sunday's liturgies; for special solemnities and functions, and for solemn events. After years of formation, and the ingrained memory of their special relationship with the Holy Father and Magisterium, Josephinum alumni will, yet again, understand what is appropriate in parish life."

All of the characteristics listed above assume that the candidate has basic relational capacity, i.e. the seminarian is able to enter into significant, even deep, relationships with other persons and with God, Since it is spiritual formation is the core that unifies the life of a priest, it stands at the heart of seminary life and is the center around which all other aspects are integrated.

6 A SOUND MIND IN A SOUND BODY

"I had spent some time studying engineering and computer science at two different state universities. But at the Josephinum, it is a much different kind of study. Before, I focused mainly on solving math problems and computer programming problems. Now I have to concentrate on reading and comprehending and synthesizing what I have learned. They are both difficult, but in different ways."
Vinhson Nguyen—Fourth Year College—Chandler AZ – [Diocese of Phoenix]

Theology isn't rocket science. It's harder. And if you don't believe that, ask any priest or seminary graduate.

It is the goal of the Josephinum to prepare seminarians who understand Divine Revelation, and who are skilled communicators able to transmit this knowledge to the faithful worldwide. Not only while resident at the Josephinum, but also in subsequent parish work, a well-rounded education is a necessity for effective ministry.

The Josephinum emphasizes the ecclesiastical aspects of the seminarians' training; namely, to be a faithful, loyal, and most importantly, an authentic teacher of the gospel. At times the workload can become daunting:

*"It can become a conflict of time management if I am not pruden-
tial with my time. However, I always have to remind myself that my*

vocation is not to become an intellectual. Although a necessary tool for priesthood, I have to remember that my academic formation cannot take over my overall spiritual formation and conformity of my life to the loving personhood of Christ." **Joseph Dalheim— Second Year Theology—Temple, TX [Diocese of Austin]**

"If I were to actually spend the time recommended to study for each class, I would have no time for anything else except maybe eating and sleeping!" **Chris Bond— First Year Theology—Cornelius, NC — [Diocese of Charlotte]**

"There are times when I have to decide what I am not going to do because I cannot do it all. Between meetings, mandatory lecturers, liturgies, other mandatory events that they spring on us, I do find myself having to decide what is going to have to be left undone." **[Joseph Finke]**

"The academic workload here takes time, just as any task does. But the intellectual dimension is a main reason why we are here, so it should take time. But it is very "doable" to balance the academic workload with the other 3 dimensions, be social, workout, and pray consistently. It is a necessary lesson to learn to operate in the busy, multitask society we live in today." **Mitchel Roman—First Year Pre-Theology— Empire MI [Diocese of Gaylord]**

"The class workload is demanding, but it is manageable. If anything, being so busy is a good way to learn time management. There are a number of other areas to which we must attend to such as Lauds (Morning prayer) and Mass beginning at 6:45 each morning. We have classes throughout the morning and sometimes in the afternoon. The afternoon is usually used to study and read. Then there is the holy hour with adoration at 4:45, which is encouraged but optional. Vespers is

required at 5:45. That is followed by dinner, attendance at which is also required. While study and intellectual formation is a main focus of our time, prayer cannot be sacrificed. We must attend to our prayer each day, and strive to be more closely conformed to Christ. It is hoped that the studies will not interfere with that, but rather enhance our goal to being more Christ like." **Michael Hartge —Third Year Theology— Reynoldsburg, OH—[Diocese of Columbus]**

Because of our unique status as a Pontifical institution, it is particularly important that seminarians at the Josephinum preach and teach in true fidelity to the Magisterium, under the authority of the Holy Father and the local diocesan Bishop to whom they will later report. Our formation program, then, emphasizes the relationship between theological knowledge and the traditions of the Catholic Church.

There is no question that the context of intellectual formation in these early years of the twenty-first century in the United States provide many challenges to both the seminary and its seminarians. For example, while many seminarians arrive with significant educational achievements, they are often quite narrowly focused; they may have great expertise or perhaps a high level of technical training, but with a rather narrow background:

"I was home schooled until 8th grade and then I attended an independent private school, run by faithful lay Catholics." **[Joseph Finke]**

"I came right out of high school." **[Blaise Radel]**

"I studied at the University of Virginia—BA Economics, French Minor" **Will Nyce—First Year Pre-Theology—Vienna, VA – [Diocese of Arlington]**

"I graduated with a degree in Finance from Concordia University in Irvine, CA" **Michael Carlson—First Year Pre-Theology—Charlotte NC—[Diocese of Charlotte]**

"Before coming to the Josephinum I graduated with a B.S. from Ohio University where I majored in Telecommunications Management. I worked for two years in broadcast radio before entering seminary. I spent a year in Nelsonville, Ohio and a year in Dallas, North Carolina." **[Michael Hartgel]**

"I completed a B.A. in both Philosophy and Theology at Franciscan University of Steubenville. Along with that, I completed all the requirements for the university's Priestly Discernment Program, which offers young men to receive intense seminary-like formation and enter into discernment of the priesthood or religious life." **[J. Michael Villanueva]**

"I graduated from a small public school called Glen Lake Community Schools in Northern Michigan in 2007. Four years later, I graduated from the small, liberal arts school, Hillsdale College (Hillsdale, MI) with a degree in Business Marketing (Marketing Management) in 2011." **[Mitchel Roman]**

Candidates frequently lack education in the humanities, which limits the effect of the study of theology, and can hinder the necessary pastoral connections to the lives of the faithful whom they later will serve.

Moreover, in recent years it has not been unusual for the Josephinum to enroll individuals with significant life experiences prior to entering the seminary. At least one physician, several lawyers and other professionals have entered as "non-traditional students" between the ages of 30 and 50 as they began their seminary journeys. While the Josephinum can make several minor adjustments, including living arrangements, academic requirements are never modified.

Institutional sensitivity to these "nontraditional students" does not indicate that seminarians from a traditional background are free from the influence of modern American culture either. Even those with well-rounded liberal arts exposure at the undergraduate level are often uncomfortable with, and suspicious of, anything which strikes of absolute moral value or objective truth. These students generally require additional work in understanding philosophical and theological anthropology, or they will remain uncomfortable with their theological studies and the application of those studies in a pastoral setting.

It is also not unusual to encounter seminarians with various levels of religious experience not only in the Catholic Church but in other denominations, as well as those seminarians with various levels of catechesis in their early lives. Seminarians have entered after secondary education in Roman Catholic high schools, in public schools, and increasingly, from a background of home schooling.

"I had never been able to study in a Catholic school before coming to seminary and have loved the ability to pray and speak about Christ openly in the classroom. Any religious education I ever had in the past came from my family." **[Vinhson Nguyen]**

"My religious education took place primarily in the CCD program at my local parish and through the instruction of my parents." **[Michael Carlson]**

"I attended Confirmation class and Catholic high school for 11th and 12th grade (and therefore, one religion class). I also participated in some

*retreats, bible studies, and continuing education seminars during and after college." [**Will Nyce**]*

*"I was quite involved with my parish's bible studies, and attended Catholic school and a Catholic university. I consider my Catholic education to have been relatively well-rounded before attending the Josephinum." [**Joseph Dalheim**]*

*"I attended parochial schools through high school. I considered myself to have a good foundation of religious education after all that, but to enter into seminary and take the undergraduate and then graduate level theology courses takes it to another level of precision. St. Charles Preparatory School here in Columbus prepared me well. That institution laid a good intellectual foundation including the study of Latin. I made use of the structure learned there in pursuing my undergraduate education. While there were a few years since studying Latin in my first two years of high school, it did make my first semester of Latin here at seminary much easier!" [**Michael Hartge**]*

In order to be as accommodating as possible the Josephinum's formation program is divided into three levels. Depending upon background and evaluation by the academic faculty, an entering seminarian may find himself in the College of Liberal Arts, Pre-Theology program, or if all prerequisites have been met, directly enrolled in the School of Theology. As an aside, it's interesting to note that until 1967 the Josephinum also included a four- year residential high school on campus, and that many of our living alumni are proud graduates of that program as well.

Faculty at the Josephinum are fortunate to have access to the latest instructional technology, both for on-site use in classrooms and through advanced distance learning platforms, although faculty preference and the nature of the material taught do limit the selection at times:

"Methods of instruction here are varied and effective. Most classes are lecture based, but enough professors/priests use visual aids and technology to help visual learners like myself." **[Chris Bond]**

"Most lessons are in the form of lectures here. It has always been difficult for my classes to be discussion based because I have such a large class. Though there have been some discussion based classes. Often PowerPoint will be used, or the professor will write on the board." [**Joseph Finke]**

"Most classes do not use PowerPoint, but rather chalk boards as visual aids. This is an effective way to teach, and sometimes the lack of technology reminds us that technology is not actually necessary, and traditionally there was no technology to learn the same material." **[Mitchel Roman]**

"I appreciate the ability of the professors here to field questions during lectures, as well as their use of visual aids, and incorporating group work into the subject matter. All of these help to better appreciate the subject matter covered." **[Joseph Dalheim]**

"Most of the instructions are lectures style, which I prefer. Only in some electives are the more seminar style in which there would be a high level of discussion. With such dense subject matter, it helps to have the lecture- style and then ask questions. The visual aids are helpful at times. The occasional video clip as a visual aid is interesting. Many teachers do use PowerPoint slides. These help with note taking as they are often posted on Populi, our in-house class network." **[Michael Hartge]**

99

The Collegiate

College programs at the Josephinum followed two major threads: humanities and philosophy. In the humanities program seminarians acquire a sense of the great questions of life as represented in the arts and sciences. This study of the natural world and of the human condition in all of history has value in its own right.

Here seminarians develop great intellectual curiosity, critical thinking, and structured and effective habits of study. They also learn communication skills which will serve them throughout their ministry. They are introduced to the wide range of human learning and experience. Through their studies of mathematics and natural sciences as well as the social and behavioral sciences as they prepare a solid foundation for the work which is to follow.

The study of languages including Latin, Greek and classical and contemporary Spanish as well as exposure to the fine arts provide an excellent grounding for their further studies of theology. These studies provide each of the seminarians with an excellent cultural understanding of the roots of their faith and its application in the 21st century. Through their study of the human sciences they begin to understand the world in which God acts and by understanding how faith and culture have interacted in the past they develop an insight into the working of God's plan and larger historical events.

The curriculum also takes into account contemporary issues of American life from an intellectual, cultural, social, economic and political perspective. Seminarians are often stimulated to deeper levels of investigation by familiarizing themselves with current events and interests. All of this is accomplished through clear presentation of the authentic teachings of the Magisterium on these issues. Students develop an appreciation of the richness and diversity of the intellectual tradition in Catholic life.

The second thread in the undergraduate programs is the study of philosophy, which is fundamental and indispensable to the later understanding of theological studies and to the formation of candidates for the priesthood.

At the Josephinum at least two full academic years are dedicated to the study of philosophy, either as a component of the undergraduate program, or in the case of those seminarians admitted after completing a undergraduate degree, in the context of a Pre-Theology program. The church recognizes the intimate bond which links the study of theology to the philosophical search for truth. Through the structured programs at the Josephinum seminarians develop an understanding of the relationship between faith and reason and the interaction between philosophy and theology.

At the Josephinum, the program of philosophy includes courses in several areas to assist students in the structured and orderly understanding of human thought. Some of these include:

- **Logic**: The study of logic helps seminarians to develop their critical and analytical abilities and become clearer thinkers who will be better able rationally to present, discuss, and defend the truths of the faith.

- **Epistemology**: The study of epistemology, the investigation of the nature and properties of knowledge, helps seminarians see that human knowledge is capable of gathering from contingent reality objective and necessary truths, while recognizing also the limits of human knowledge. Moreover, it reinforces their understanding of the relationship between reason and revelation. They come to appreciate the power of reason to know the truth, and yet, as they confront the limits of the powers of human reason, they are opened to look to revelation for a fuller knowledge of those truths that exceed the power of human reason.

- **Philosophy of Nature**: The study of the philosophy of nature, which treats fundamental principles like substance, form, matter, causality, motion, and the soul, provides seminarians a foundation for the study of metaphysics, natural theology, anthropology, and ethics.

- **Metaphysics**: The study of metaphysics helps seminarians explore fundamental issues concerning the nature of reality and see that reality and truth transcend the empirical. Philosophy which shuns metaphysics would be radically unsuited to the task of mediation in the understanding of revelation.

- **Natural Theology**: The study of natural theology, which treats the existence of God and the attributes of God by means of the natural light of reason, provides a foundation for the seminarian's study of theology and the knowledge of God by means of revelation.

- **Philosophical Anthropology**: The study of philosophical anthropology helps seminarians explore the authentic spirituality of man, leading to a theocentric ethic, transcending earthly life, and at the same time open to the social dimension of man.

- **Ethics:** The study of ethics, which treats general principles of ethical decision making, provides seminarians with a solid grounding in themes like conscience, freedom, law, responsibility, virtue, and guilt. Ethics also considers the common good and virtue of solidarity as central to Christian social political philosophy. It provides a foundation for the seminarian's study of moral theology.

Josephinum collegians seem to respond well to the challenges of the undergraduate program, although not all see the program in the same light:

"If I knew how intense philosophy was I would have paid much more attention in my high school classes and also I wish I studied Latin Grammar and also Euclid." **[Blaise Radel]**

"I actually thought the academics here would be harder. I expected them to be better. For that matter I still expect them to be better. There are times where I feel that I am wasting my time. That is not to say that there is not a large enough work load, because there is, but the content of the lectures, tests, and homework often times could be more challenging." **[Joseph Finke]**

But in all of the college courses the Josephinum gives full recognition to the seminal works of St. Thomas Aquinas. Especially in the courses on the history of philosophy there is a significant treatment of St. Thomas' thought, along with its ancient sources and its later development. The fruitful relationship between philosophy and theology in the Christian tradition are explored through studies in Thomistic thought as well as that of other great Christian theologians who were also great philosophers. These include certain Fathers of the Church, medieval doctors, and recent Christian thinkers in the Western and Eastern traditions.

Undergraduate Theology

At the Josephinum college level study begins with the study of theology with undergraduate courses which focus on the fundamental beliefs and practices the Catholic faith. These concentrate on those elements of the faith that perhaps had been overlooked or neglected in the the seminarians earlier religious education and which may he considered a per-supposition for the materials covered in the graduate theological study.

These courses begin with the themes contained in the catechism of the Catholic Church, with particular emphasis on Catholic doctrine, liturgy and the sacraments, morality, prayer, and sacred Scripture. By the time these courses have been successfully completed, all Josephinum seminarians have a solid knowledge of the catechism and its contents as a source for a full and complete exposition of Catholic doctrine.

Additionally at the Josephinum, international seminarians have an opportunity to learn English and study the culture of the United States as a prelude to their preparation for priestly ministry at the the School of Theology. It is here especially that these international students study the history of the United States, its culture and its language, to supplement the seminarians previous educational experiences as a background for preparation for graduate-level study of theology.

Pre-Theology

The Pre-Theology program prepares Josephinum seminarians who have completed college but lack the philosophical and theological background and other areas necessary to pursue graduate-level theology. The study of philosophy, as outlined above, is central to the academic formation of all students in this program.

Education in rhetoric and communications as well as appropriate language study are also contained in the Pre-Theology programs. Special emphasis is placed upon Latin and Greek. The study of Spanish or other languages used in a pastoral setting are included in the curriculum as appropriate. But regardless of which courses are undertaken, the intellectual formation of seminarians at the Josephinum is a search for ever deepening knowledge of the divine mysteries.

Pre-theologians, when asked what changes they would have made in their undergraduate education before entering the Josephinum — perhaps because of their life-experiences and greater maturity — seem to be more accepting of their classroom experiences:

"I would be less stressed about classes, knowing the four dimensions need to be balanced equally and that the faculty and teachers are here to help you succeed at both you academics and your other responsibilities as long as you put in the effort." **[Mitchel Roman]**

"I would have completed 90% of all 'personal reading and study' before the semester started!" **[Michael Carlson]**

The Theologate

The Josephinum's School of Theology is a four year program. It requires appropriate and sound philosophical formation. As a result, it complements both the Collegiate program and Pre-Theology programs offered at the Josephinum.

Because of the essential nature of the mission of the School of Theology, all professors are required to make a profession of faith and have a canonical mission. The academic program, which has a discernible and coherent unity, allows the seminarian to develop a clear understanding of the ministerial priesthood. Central to the curriculum is a detailed study of fundamental theology, which is the basis of the rational process of all theology, and which thus serves as an appropriate introduction to subsequent courses of study.

Also critical to the entire curriculum is a study of sacred Scripture as foundational, and as the logical entry point to further studies in theology. Specific courses at the Josephinum include the study of the Pentateuch, the historical and prophetic and wisdom books of the Old Testament with emphasis upon the Psalms, the synoptic Gospels and the Acts, Pauline and Johannine literature and the Epistles utilizing an historical-critical method in conjunction with other synchronic approaches to unlock the riches contained in the biblical texts. Particular emphasis is placed upon the interpretation of Scripture so that seminarians have a solid grounding when preaching homilies and applying Scripture to the life of the faithful.

Patristic studies are essential part of the theology curriculum. These draw from the works of the fathers of the Church and have a lasting value within the living tradition of the faith community. In dogmatic theology, Josephinum seminarians study the theology of God, Christiology, creation, the fall and the nature of sin, redemption, grace and the human person, ecclesiology, sacraments, eschatology, Mariology, and Pastoral Theology.

A separate and detailed course of study concerning Holy Orders, with emphasis upon the nature and mission of the ministerial priesthood, including a history and theology of celibacy, is also required of Josephinum seminarians.

The curriculum provides a thorough study of contents and methods of catechesis to prepare the seminarian for his task as a minister of the Word and also provides synthesis linking and unified the other courses in the program.

Courses in moral theology including fundamental moral theology, moral ethics, sexual morality and social ethics, are taught based upon Sacred Scripture and tradition, references to the natural law and absolute moral norms and provide consideration to the results of the natural and human sciences. In these courses, the close link between moral, spiritual and dogmatic theology is evident. The pastoral tasks of the seminarians after ordination to the priesthood as ministers of the sacrament of penance are emphasized here.

Experience has taught us that the importance of a clear understanding of the principles of medical and moral ethics are critical for seminarians ordained into contemporary culture. Seminarians learn and practice the fundamental respect for human life from conception to natural death and understand the moral dangers of and pastoral methods of addressing contraception, abortion and euthanasia.

The program of theology at the Josephinum is thorough in its presentation of the authentic teachings of the church in regards to sexual moral matters. It presumes a mature biological and basic scientific social scientific understanding of human sexuality. This is a matter of special importance since the seminarian's formation in celibate chastity includes the intellectual assent to, and embrace of the church's moral teachings on these topics.

The social teachings of the church are presented in their entirety with particular emphasis upon the systematic study of the social encyclicals of the popes. In addition, considerable emphasis is placed upon the professional ethics appropriate to pastoral ministry.

The theological curriculum at the Josephinum includes courses on the history of the church universal and the history of the Catholic Church in the United States. These courses reflect the multicultural origins and ecumenical context as well. These historical courses include the study of patristics and the lives of the Saints.

The Pontifical College Josephinum is particularly proud of our expertise in Canon Law. The *Bishop James Griffith Chair in Canon Law* has been established in honor of the former Bishop of the Diocese of Columbus, who also served for many years as the Josephinum's Vice-Chancellor, by a number of benefactors including priests of the diocese. These courses include introductions to Canon law, Canon law relating to various sacraments, and provide special relevance to Book Two (the people of God) and Book Five (the temporal goods of the church).

Courses are also offered in various areas of spirituality. These courses address the Catholic spiritual tradition, and provide practical directives for the Christian call to perfection as well as principles of discernment for the individual. These also explore the spirituality of various vocations, especially the priesthood and consecrated life.

Liturgical studies include an examination of the theological, historical, pastoral, and judicial aspects of Catholic liturgy. Seminarians learn to celebrate all of the church's sacred rites according to the mind and heart of the Church.

Seminarians practice the celebration of the Eucharist and the other sacraments, with particular attention given to the practicum for the sacrament of penance. At the Josephinum seminarians are introduced to the official liturgical books used by the clergy, and to current directives concerning music, art and architecture in a liturgical setting.

The Josephinum places great emphasis upon homiletics, which is integrated in the entire course of studies. In addition to the principles of biblical interpretation, catechesis and communications theory, seminarians learn the practical skills necessary to communicate the Gospels effectively. They are also afforded opportunities to preach outside of Eucharistic celebrations and receive formal assessment They also deliver homilies in the Spanish language, and are assessed appropriately.

Courses in ecumenism address the Catholic Church's commitment to the principles and fundamental roles of ecumenical dialogue, as well as current ecumenical issues.

Finally, as men approach ordination, they generally express deeper understanding, appreciation and acceptance of the educational and developmental processes which they had undertaken for the past several years. When asked the traditional question beloved of social scientists (If you knew then what you know now...) there was significant congruity in their responses:

"I would be less worried about the academics at seminary. I thought they might try to drown us with academics... but it was more balanced than I expected. It is clear to me that they understand that academics, while necessary, is not the be all and end all. It must be integrated with the three other dimensions of formation as well." [J. **Michael Villanueva**]

"I would not have been nearly as nervous or anxious. The faculty (especially the lay faculty in teaching the philosophy courses) are ready to do whatever they can to help seminarians outside of class to gain a better grasp on the subject matter. They don't set you up for failure or leave you adrift. You only have to apply yourself and seek assistance when needed. They want you to succeed and to be able to freely discern

God's call in your life. You're not in this alone when you enter semi-nary. There are many to help you discern the will of the Lord in your life. Most importantly Christ is right there with you. If He wants you to be his priest, He will bring his work to completion. The seminarians merely have to use the gifts He has given them and rely on His grace for the rest!" **[Michael Hartge]**

At the Josephinum, because of our absolute loyalty to the Magisterium of the church, this theology is studied in complete and faithful communion with the teaching authority of the Holy Father. This flows from the prayer of Christ for his flock and the renewed vision of the Second Vatican Council, and is far from being exclusive as an ecumenical imperative. It is a process and not an event, and serves as an initiation into a lifelong study of the truths of faith. Both the faculty and seminarians recognize the criticality of balance among the four dimensions of priestly formation and guard against the temptation to over-intellectualize what is, in its most essential form, a willing acceptance of God's call to ordination.

The Josephinum as been honored by its status as a fully accredited educational institution, not only by the Association of Theological Schools of Canada and the United States (ATS) but also by the North Central Association of Colleges and Schools. First accredited by ATS in 1970, the most recent and successful re-accreditation visits by both groups occurred in the fall of 2012.

7 FORMATION FOR EFFECTIVE MINISTRY

"The liturgies which I've experienced at the Josephinum have been very reverent and direct the mind towards God. One thing that makes our liturgies so beautiful is the great liturgical music we have from multiple choirs." **Daniel Rice—First Year College—Chantilly,Va—[Diocese of Arlington]**

Because all four dimensions of formation are interdependent, at the Josephinum pastoral formation rightly complements the entire formative process. It is in response to the grace of Holy Orders that, once ordained, a seminarian stands and acts in the community in the name of Jesus Christ.

It is incumbent then, that this sacramental character be fulfilled by the personal and pastoral formation of the seminarian. In this way, he will be able to effectively communicate the mysteries of faith through his human personality as a bridge and witness the faith rooted in these spiritual life and express his knowledge of faith.

While these imperatives converge in pastoral formation, the grace to be a true shepherd comes through ordination. This grace, however, calls for the seminarian's personal commitment to develop both the knowledge and the skills required of a teacher and preacher, to celebrate the sacraments prayerfully, and to respond to the needs of the faithful as well as to take initiatives which his priesthood requires. Pastoral formation, then, focuses upon a number of essential elements:

Celebration of the Sacraments is central to the ministry of the priest. Although a seminarian cannot yet celebrate the sacraments in the manner of the priest, he can accompany priests who do and can prepare those who participate in those sacraments. Even in his earliest days he can begin to develop a sense of what sacramental ministry entails. He begins to appreciate the sacraments role in the salvation of souls and understands how the sacraments, most especially the Eucharist, nurture God's people. And no liturgy is more important and more valued by the seminarians than the Mass:

"Liturgy is always a point of interest for any seminarian. Because of that a lot of effort goes into making sure that liturgies at the Josephinum are conducted well, in a manner that befits what we are worshiping. Seeing all the work that goes in behind the scenes has given me a great deal of respect for liturgy at the Josephinum." **Daniel Swartz—Second Year Theology—Columbus Ohio—[Diocese of Columbus]**

"The liturgy here is excellent! My dad, upon visiting, remarked, 'That Mass had everything in it that you could put into a Mass, but with no wasted time! You've got this down to a science.' The liturgy at the PCJ is very beautiful and executed with such rigorous precision that some students have even begun to wonder if liturgical rules have been over emphasized, to the detriment of formation in other areas of the gospel. This is something of a cultural question amongst the seminarians. In my view - and I think Pope Francis is a good witness to this principle on an even broader level - as long as we keep Jesus Christ at the center of what we do, we will be on the right track. The Church requires some flexibility, as surely as she provides the objective truth which defines

*its parameters. For my own part, I am proud to be part of a genera-
tion of young Catholics who want to take the liturgy - especially the
Holy Sacrifice of the Mass - seriously! There is nothing more important
than to receive Christ in the Eucharist, and to do this well means to be
attentive in how we as (future) pastors will celebrate the Mass."* **Josh
Altonji— First Year Theology—Huntsville, AL—[Diocese of
Birmingham]**

*"The liturgies have been integral to my formation as a pastor. I realize
the importance of beautiful liturgy in order to bring people to a greater
worship of God. The liturgical practices here have been very orthodox
and formative in my understanding of the different liturgical seasons
and practices. I see how liturgical practices should be done in the mind
of the Church and I have become more sensitive to the importance
of implementing orthodox worship in parishes."* **Edward Shikina—
Fourth Year—Pre-Theology—Columbus Ohio—[Diocese of
Columbus]**

*"The liturgies at the Josephinum are some of the best I've experienced in
terms of reverence, music selections, and overall quality. The program of
liturgy is well-balanced, with opportunities to attend the Extraordinary
Form Mass, the Latin Novus Ordo Mass, and Mass in Spanish."*
**Christopher Hamilton— Second Year Pre-Theology—Gastonia
NC—[Diocese of Charlotte]**

*"The liturgies at the Josephinum have not infrequently been lovely, mys-
terious, and awe-inspiring. They have been the most solemn liturgies I
have experienced, and the first time I felt a sense of awe and mystery at
Mass."* **Timothy Davis— Second Year Pre-Theology— Chadwick
IL —[Diocese of Santa Fe]**

Proclamation of the Word: Pastoral formation emphasizes the proclamation of Scripture, a primary obligation of the

113

priest. This ministry is directed toward the conversion of sinners. It is built upon the seminarian's ability to listen sincerely and to understand the living experiences and the realities of the faithful. This listening then is followed by the priest's ability to interpret these experiences in the light of Scripture and of the church's traditions. The seminarian must couple his personal convictions of faith with the continuing development of his communication skills so that Scripture may be effectively expressed. This extends to the optional forms of the Eucharistic Celebration, as well as to the liturgical formats of the various rites which are in communion with Rome:

> *I have served the Extraordinary Form of the Mass, and I have been a Lector for morning prayer and Mass. I have fulfilled the role of sacristan at a local parish at home during the week. I have been Master of Ceremonies at my home parish as well as having been Lector, subdeacon, and organist/choir director.* **David Freundl— First Year College –Traverse City MI —[Diocese of Gaylord]**

> *"I have attended the Extraordinary form of the Roman Rite. I have also experience Byzantine and Maronite liturgies."* **[Daniel Swartz]**

> *"I too have participated in the Extraordinary Form of the Mass, the Eastern Rite, as well as the Catholic Anglican Ordinariate."* **[Christopher Hamilton]**

> *"The Josephinum celebrates the Extraordinary Form once or twice a month, and on breaks we are encouraged to visit Eastern Rite Churches, which I have done. I would like to see a consistent implementation of the Vatican II Constitution Sacrosanctum Concilium: consistent use of Latin, chant, ad orientam celebrations of the Mass, etc. I also long for an opportunity to assist at the Extraordinary Form of the Mass"* **[Timothy Davis]**

"I have attended the Extraordinary Form of the Mass since being here. It allows for a good reflection on how the Church has historically talked about the liturgy. I have extensive experience with the Byzantine Rite, both according to the Ruthenian and Melkite recensions, and I have attended Divine Liturgy in the Coptic and Syro-Malabar rites on my own time." **Thomas Herge—-First Year Pre-Theology—Columbus Ohio—[Diocese of Columbus]**

Thirdly, all priests are missionaries of heart. The church is an evangelizing church. At the Josephinum seminarians have many opportunities to become aware of the work of the pontifical mission societies, and missionary congregations of religious. Indeed throughout the history of the Josephinum members of many of the societies have participated both as students and faculty. This day- to-day exposure to the missionary church has been of enormous benefit to the seminarians at the Josephinum.

In a related arena, pastoral formation introduces seminarians to the care and guidance and leadership that the church extends to the local community. In the United States of the 21st century, exhibition of individualism is all too common. It is the role of the pastor to primarily focus on the community at large and then on individuals within that community.

There are specific skills which are useful, and indeed required, for effective pastoral care. The ability to communicate the mysteries of faith clearly and an easily comprehensible terms, using appropriate media is critical. But greater than the "trade school" skills—pastoral formation signifies a level of commitment to personal development which is fitting for the priest to speak in the name of Jesus Christ. Pastoral formation for public ministry demands flexibility of spirit that enables the newly ordained priest to relate to people of many different cultures and theological and ecclesiastical persuasions. Proper pastoral formation assists the seminarian to put on both the mind and heart of Christ when dealing with the greater world. Josephinum seminarians have well- founded considerations about liturgy, as well as experience with a number of liturgical roles:

"I have been Thurifer,* Lector and Acolyte. We have many opportunities to serve in different capacities at Mass, the Liturgy of the Hours, and Holy Hour. I have been an altar server since I have been in middle school. Serving Mass as a child and through high school has helped give me a liturgical sense as we serve more now in seminary. It is also a privilege to serve as Master of Ceremonies for our bishop throughout the diocese. It's a great way to spend time with the bishop and to meet the priests and faithful of the diocese." **Michael Hartge —Third Year Theology—Reynoldsburg, OH—[Diocese of Columbus]**

"Liturgical formation is critical to the New Evangelization, since a beautiful, noble liturgy exalts the mind and fills the soul with love for Our Lord, giving us the strength and inspiration to reach out to our neighbor in love, and it is essential for preparing the soul to encounter Christ in the Blessed Sacrament. Pre-theologians are trained as Server and Thurifer for the daily Adoration of the Blessed Sacrament, and this has been both beautiful and moving. I sometimes have served as an Acolyte and Lector at my home parish and on summer assignment." **[Timothy Davis]**

"I've been Server and Thurifer at Adoration. The Josephinum does a great job of easing you into the different roles. I've also served as Lector and Acolyte at a parish in my diocese, and even helped distribute the Body and the Blood." **[Richard Childress]**

"I would not mind being able to sing Compline nightly, but certainly not as a mandatory thing. I have been Thurifer at holy hour, and I

have sung in the polyphonic choir. I have been a Server for years at my home parish, but in various places I have been a reader, extraordinary minister of Holy Communion, and I act as Master of Ceremonies for our bishop." **[Thomas Herge]**

"I think the Josephinum could help us contact other rites of Catholicism so that we could better appreciate the diversity and complimentary aspects of our religious practices. It would be cool to participate in a Mass they would have in India or Russia, especially if we were given the opportunity to be walked through it before-hand so that we could understand the Theology behind it. Also, it would be nice to celebrate a true Hispanic Mass. My first year here, the Spanish Mass was accompanied by a Marachi band. While I don't think it is exactly conducive to post-Mass prayer and reflection, it is something more true to the real world and a cultural context in which we may one day be placed. If anything, it will aid us in empathy so we can better serve God's people in the future. My most frequent liturgical duty is that of Cantoring, but I've also thoroughly enjoyed Lectoring and serving." **Joey Collopy—Fourth Year College—Ft.Thomas, Ky.—[Diocese of Covington]**

It is sometimes useful to view pastoral formation as a process which links the elements of human, spiritual and intellectual formation so that they can be put to practical use for the faithful, especially in a parish context. At the Josephinum seminarians experience parish internships which provide an opportunity to link is parish experiences and discern how his seminary formation can make a difference. As a homilist, the deacon in a transitional year, for example, revisits his formation and now has an opportunity to see it through the lens of practical realities.

Seminarians at the Josephinum have multiple opportunities for practical pastoral exposure: field placements, common pastoral internships, or clinical pastoral education in a hospital setting. They do not function alone as there is always a guide, a mentor or a teacher ready to accompany the seminarian and to help him learn from his experience.

The Josephinum's Director of Pastoral Formation assists the seminarian in understanding the priestly dimension of these experiences. Ideally, the seminarian first arrives as an observer, then seeks to understand from more experienced participants what he is seeing, then generates a series of questions as to what is actually occurring, and finally integrates the experience into his formation. Ideally, he then becomes a participant- observer and attempts to do whatever the situation requires. His theological reflection provides an opportunity for personal synthesis, the understanding of motivations, and further appreciation of the pastoral role in life and ministry. The Director of Pastoral Formation, acting in the name of the Rector/President ensures that the sacramental dimension of pastoral care is foremost in any such program in which Josephinum's seminarians are active.

"I have served in a variety of capacities for St. Joseph Parish in Plain City, assisted St. Paul's Outreach at OSU, taught at St. Charles High School, and worked at St. Paul Parish in Westerville with the youth group, the Catholics Come Home program, and now at the elementary school. In the summer, I have worked in parishes in the Diocese of Alexandria, assisting vacation bible schools, altar server training, funerals, weddings, baptisms, and even helped renovate an old school building into a new community center." **Brian Seiler— Third Year Theology—Alexandria, LA —[Diocese of Alexandria]**

"Since I am new this year, I have only done Hispanic RCIA at a local parish since coming to the Josephinum. Before arriving here, however,

I did a wide plethora of pastoral ministry: Confirmation prep, jail ministry, Catholic Charities, retired-priest ministry, nursing home visits, hospital chaplaincy, and assisting at the diocesan office. I've also worked in Catholic Charities, and helped out at the diocesan office."
Joseph Dalheim— Second Year Theology—Temple, TX [Diocese of Austin]

"Last summer, I participated in a program called Totus Tuus with the Nashville diocese in which I was able to join a team of four college-aged missionaries in teaching both kids and teens at various parishes in a week-long summer program. It was a bit like being a school teacher, a camp counselor, a little league coach, a liturgist, a DRE, a youth minister, and an itinerant preacher all at once! The program itself was excellent, and provided the youth of each parish with a solid sacramental catechesis, lots of laughs, and a good exposure to young Catholic role models (the missionaries). We had water balloon fights, crazy skits, and silly songs with the kids, but also serious small-group conversations, Eucharistic adoration, and faith-sharing talks with the teens. It was not an experience I would trade for anything, and I am absolutely ecstatic that my own diocese - Birmingham, AL - will be picking up the program for the first time this summer, and I will most likely be reprising my role as a missionary!

The greatest and most unexpected benefit for me as a seminarian in this program was the incredible formation that it gave me in the area of daily prayer. Every day on a Totus Tuus team is a day of intense prayer and work, but when we pray we pray together. Every day as a team we would have Morning and Evening Prayer, the rosary, a divine mercy chaplet, Mass with the kids, Night Prayer with the teens, and various devotional prayers throughout the day. This experience was incredibly helpful for my spiritual growth, because I noticed such an increase in my joy and my faith as a result of these grace-filled days of prayer that I determined to keep saying most of these prayers on my own, for the

119

rest of the summer and on into the school year. Even today, six months later, the habit of praying the rosary and divine mercy chaplet I began as a Totus Tuus missionary help form the backbone of my daily prayer life at seminary.

On a pastoral note, my experience as a missionary in the Totus Tuus program really helped to strengthen my sense of vocation as a priest, not only because each week ended with a "Vocations Panel" for the teens where priests and religious (and married couples!) shared their vocation stories with us, but even more so because of the opportunity the summer program provided me for living a life of full-time ministry and leading others in sacramental worship. Obviously I was not "saying Mass" every day, but I was helping to bring the kids to Jesus in a very concrete way! There is also something very pastoral - very shepherd-like - about having to corral 50-100 kids every morning! It is an intense life to be sure, but it is a life of love. I also became very familiar with the seven parishes that my team worked at over the course of the summer, and formed relationships with the host families who gave us food and shelter during the week. I therefore highly recommend the Totus Tuus missionary program to seminarians not only as an opportunity for ministry and for spiritual growth, but also as a way to truly be <u>with</u> people in a pastoral context, in a way that is not always possible even at a typical summer assignment in a parish."
Josh Altonji— First Year Theology—Huntsville, AL—[Diocese of Birmingham]

"I have assisted at a religion class last year, and this current year I am helping teach RCIA. In my previous (and first) summer assignment, I assisted at Mass, worked with children at a Vacation Bible School program, assisted parishioners who visited the sick and home-bound, and became involved with the youth and young adult groups of the parish."
[Timothy Davis]

"Last year I helped stock shelves at the Our Lady of Guadalupe Center. That experience helped me understand much better the workings and needs of food pantries. This year I have been involved with high school youth ministry. Having begun small groups every other week, I have been struck by the kids' faith, and leading them deeper into the mystery of Christ has been exciting and humbling. I had worked in a small parish away from the city my first year. Last year I helped at a suburban parish and commuted to work half-time at Catholic Charities' Join Organization for Inner-City Needs (JOIN). That latter experience I really wish could have been full-time. Getting to know the wonderful people who work there was invaluable, but interviewing those in need, seeing in them the face of Christ, and treating them like human beings, sometimes to their bewilderment, was transformative for me." **[Thomas Hergel]**

In recent years increased emphasis has been placed upon the multicultural realities of the church in North America. Seminarians continue to develop a deeply-rooted appreciation of the diversity which marks the Catholic Church in 21st century America. Seminarians have been exposed to many cultures and languages, not only in the local diocese, but in summer placements in their home diocese and elsewhere. Through practical experience, they learn how to welcome migrants and refugees pastorally, liturgically, and culturally. They develop an ability to assist newcomers to adapt themselves into the mainstream as seamlessly as possible. Through their activities, they also develop a keen appreciation for religious pluralism. They learn how to work within the ecumenical and interfaith communities that form a backdrop for life in the United States and for the Catholic Church in North America.

Critical to the development of seminarians at the Josephinum is a clear understanding of the needs of the seminarian's home diocese.

The Josephinum takes particular care to ensure cordial and productive relationships with those local priests with whom the seminarian will be workers in cooperation with the Bishop. Seminarians are encouraged to cultivate communion with, and to learn how to serve,the diocese to which they will ultimately be assigned. The Josephinum strives to ensure that seminarians understand the future pastoral assignments as something wider than their own preference or interests, but rather as a sharing in the far wider vision of the universal church.

For seminarians to be true followers of the model of Jesus Christ, they must have sustained contact with those most underprivileged in the eye of God; namely the poor, the marginalized, the sick and the suffering. Through these encounters they learn to cultivate a preferential opinion of the poor and learn to beware of the social context and structures which can breed injustice. The Josephinum continually strives to form seminarians who can develop and implement ways to provide greater justice and social structures:

"I have been on multiple mission trips to help in the mountains south of Oaxaca, Mexico before coming to seminary. In my time in seminary, I have been on a mission trip to El Salvador with PCJ seminarians and Ohio Dominican students and I have attended the PCJ Spanish immersion program and mission service project in Cuernavaca, Mexico. Outside of mission trips, I have not had the opportunity to do pastoral work in my non-predominant language, but the Josephinum is training me through the Hispanic Ministry course to be prepared to do so after ordination." **[Brian Seiler]**

"I have participated in two different mission trips. Bringing financial and spiritual support to (1) remote villages in Guatemala and (2) poor communities in coastal Mexico. I've also worked with General Cepeda, Mexico with Family Missions Co. and Valle de Los

Angeles Orphanage (run by OFM Franciscans) in the remote areas of Guatemala. I have participated in a Mission Trip to Lourdes, France and even a local mission trip to downtown Steubenville, Ohio. Each overseas mission trip that I listed required use of Spanish! I especially loved the mission trip in Lourdes... not only did I get to use my Spanish to speak to others... I got to translate for the rest of my group!" **J. Michael Villanueva—First Year Theology—Anthem, AZ— [Diocese of Phoenix]**

"I have worked with youth groups, as a Catholic Youth Summer Camp counselor and with men's faith groups. I've brought communion to the sick and elderly, held a book discussion group, and worked at an orphanage in Kenya. My orphanage work in Kenya was not traditional mission work but it was as a conscious part of my future pastoral work that I volunteered there." **Edward Shikina—Fourth Year Pre-Theology—Columbus, OH—[Diocese of Columbus]**

"I was afforded the opportunity to teach English at a minor/major seminary in the holy land for a year. I was able to 'mix' in some Arabic at the Patriarchal seminary there." **Will Nyce—First Year Pre-Theology—Vienna, VA – [Diocese of Arlington]**

At the Josephinum seminarians also learn a dimension of practical administration. The program includes an opportunity for seminarians to acquire those basic administrative skills necessary for pastors or pastoral associates. Indeed, courses in pastoral administration are among the most popular and successful offerings developed at the Josephinum in recent years. Seminarians learn to manage the physical and financial resources of a parish, with particular emphasis upon educating parishioners about the gospel value of stewardship, and developing an ability to organize parish life effectively to achieve diocesan goals.

Neither is the collaborative nature of modern ministry is overlooked at the Josephinum. Within the seminary itself, seminarians interact with lay men and women as professors and staff as well as representatives of a number of religious communities. Particularly in light of the reduced numbers of ordained clergy experienced over the last forty years, parish life in the United States as been blessed with many people who serve —permanent deacons, members of religious communities both male and female, professionally trained lay ministers – and volunteers and members of both parish and diocesan consultative bodies. To work well with this panoply of God's faithful, the newly ordained priest must hone his personal skills and qualities. These qualities include a sense of responsibility for initiating and following through complex tasks, a well-developed spirit of collaboration, skill in conflict resolution, and, most importantly, a flexibility of spirit to enable him to make adjustments for new and unexpected circumstances.

The Josephinum has been fortunate for many years with the quality and zeal of those priests and laity who supervise the pastoral formation of our seminarians. To willingly assume such responsibility requires a great deal of experience, competence and generosity of spirit. The willingness of bishops and religious supervisors to make such individuals available for extended periods of time has always been a key to the success of the Josephinum, making it a true national and international resource for the education of new priests. The priests and others who have been made available to the Josephinum have always exhibited personal qualities which include fierce devotion to priestly formation, patience, and an instinctive way of thinking theologically about the pastoral mission as well as a habit of prayer which permeates everything which they do. And they do so with a great sense of good humor and humility.

Finally, every seminarian at the Pontifical College Josephinum is accorded the opportunity to actively witness to the Church's firm commitment to the sanctity of human life, as well as participate in the New Evangelization, and most do so with a fervor which is truly awe-inspiring:

"I have attended the March for Life and the mass in the armory and participated in the One Gospel events of St. Paul's Outreach at Ohio State." **[Brian Seiler]**

"I have done regular sidewalk prayer ministry at a local abortion clinic since entering seminary. I have also regularly attended the March for Life in DC to witness to life as well." **[Joseph Dalheim]**

"I went on the March for Life both in 2013 and 2014. Being able to pray with the brothers as we march, especially in the cold and the snow, is an amazing experience." **[Thomas Hergel]**

"There is nothing that gives me more hope for the Church or more pride in being a PCJ seminarian than the high level of involvement that our seminarians have in various pro-life activities. The outstanding level of attendance we have for the March for Life in D.C. is just the tip of the iceberg.

Every Saturday morning - rain or shine, snow or ice - two shifts of seminarians go out to pray in front of the abortion mill on Cleveland Avenue. (The other one we prayed at last year closed down, praise God!) We do not typically hold signs - obnoxious or otherwise - but we do hold our rosaries as we ask our blessed mother Mary's intercession to heal the hearts of those wounded by abortion. We pray not only for the lives of the unborn and for their salvation, but also for hope and healing for young mothers, for their families, for those who have to live with the guilt or loss of an aborted child in their family, and for the culture of life to be realized through just legislation that protects every person regardless of age and ability.

We also have a vibrant PJHL (Peace, Justice, and Human Life) committee, which provides a way for many seminarians to assume leadership in areas pertaining to social justice. The club is thus "pro-life" in the broadest sense, not only partnering with 40 Days for Life and local crisis pregnancy centers, but also sponsoring an annual St. Stephen's Day party and gift drive for underprivileged children, promoting awareness of human rights abuses in the news, forming seminarians with respect to Church teaching about the dignity of human life, and seeking new ways to assist those in need.

Finally, I have been blessed to be involved with a relatively new seminarian-led ministry called the New Evangelization Club, which was started last year by my classmate, Stephen Vaccaro. We actually get a lot of jokes that we are "like the Mormons", because we go door-to-door with members of a local parish sharing the gospel message to people in Columbus. (I prefer to think that we are like the apostles!) This year we will be expanding our outreach to include the Ohio State University campus, where we will partner with existing Catholic student ministries to share the gospel with their classmates. These types of experiences can seem intimidating to be sure, and Jesus spoke truly when he said that our evangelical efforts would not always be appreciated, but the experience and the vulnerability of going door to door has been a powerful spiritual experience for me. Like the pro-life movement, this sort of work provides me with an opportunity to stand up in the midst of seeming adversity for the sake of the gospel, strengthening in turn my own dependence upon the Holy Spirit for spiritual strength to do that which is difficult but also necessary. Most surprisingly, going door to door has also provided an occasion for many joyful and even heart-warming experiences with people who may or may not be Catholic, but were kind enough to offer a welcoming smile and a pleasant conversation to the Catholic missionaries standing at their door! If there is a moral here, it is this: do not be afraid to share the gospel! The faith was never meant to be a private or selfish affair. Be brave; be generous." Josh Altonji— First Year Theology—Huntsville, AL—[Diocese of Birmingham]

Well said, Mr. Altonji, well said, indeed. We'll look at the most recent March for Life in Washington D.C. in greater detail in our next chapter.

* Thurifer. The Acolyte who carries and uses the Navicula (the boat shaped vessel containing incense) and uses the incense filled Thurible during liturgical activities.

GALLERY TWO

Procession entering St. Turibius Chapel for Sunday Mass. The grandeur and solemnity of liturgical worship is a characteristic of life at the Josephinum, the only Pontifical Seminary in North America.

[Photo credit: Carolyn Dinovo/Josh Altonji – PCJ]

Deacons Richard Vu, Terry McGowen, Brian Medlin, Juan Salazar, and Michael Hennigan participate in a solemn pontifical liturgy during their pre-ordination visit to the Vatican in 2013.

[Photo credit: Carolyn Dinovo/Josh Altonji – PCJ]

Father Joseph A. Murphy SJ, STD long-serving Associate Professor of Theology's lectures are always well attended by collegians and theologians alike.

[Photo credit: Carolyn Dinovo/Josh Altonji – PCJ]

Doctor Perry Cahall lectures to theologians in the spacious and newly renovated audio-visual lecture hall. The Josephinum is a recognized leader in advanced instructional media including a very robust distance learning network as part of its extension services initiative.

[Photo credit: Carolyn Dinovo/Josh Altonji – PCJ]

Seminarian Mark Simpson with the children of Cuernavaca. Mexico. Jesus said, "Let the children come to me, and do not prevent them; for the kingdom of heaven belongs to such as these." (Mat. 19:14)

[Photo credit: Dr. Dale Meade- PCJ]

Seminarian Anthony Stewart (on ladder) works with the local church while on the mission visit to Cuernavaca, Fr. John Rozembajgier the Dean of Seminary Life for the College stands in doorway.

[Photo credit: Dr. Dale Meade- PCJ]

Seminarians Jonathan Eichold and Alex Kowalkowski during the 2014 March for Life in Washington.
[Photo credit: Josh Altonji – PCJ]

The contingent from the Pontifical College /Josephinum with the U.S. Capital in the
background, January,[Photo credit: Josh Altonji – PCJ] 2014
[Photo credit: Josh Altonji – PCJ]

Josephinum Alumni at the Bi-Annual Reunion in 2012.
[Photo credit: Carolyn Dinovo – PCJ]

8 THE MARCH FOR LIFE IN WASHINGTON

"The March for Life is a dichotomy for a Christian and more so for a Catholic seminarian. On the one hand there is the obvious somber and harrowing reality that we gather in great numbers to stand against the slaughter of innocent youth in our country. The other side, though, is one of joy and hope. So many young and vibrant Catholic youth, priests, religious, and all manner of lay organizations stand together; it is a great testament to the strength and unity of the Church." **Daniel Swartz—Second Year Theology—Columbus Ohio— [Diocese of Columbus]**

For the Roman Catholic Church, there is no distinction between defending human life and promoting the dignity of the human person.

As a gift from God, every human life is sacred from conception to natural death. The life and dignity of every person must be respected and protected at every stage and in every condition. The right to life is the first and most fundamental principle of human rights that leads Catholics to actively work for a world of greater respect for human life and greater commitment to justice and peace.

This long-held tenant of moral theology has been challenged by the climate of abortion recently, particularly in light of the infamous

Roe v. Wade decision of the United States Supreme Court in January 1973.

Both the Supreme Pontiff and the American bishops have spoken clearly and forcefully in opposition to this climate of permissiveness in regards to the life of the unborn child:

"The inviolability of the person which is a reflection of the absolute inviolability of God, finds its primary and fundamental expression in the inviolability of human life. Above all, the common outcry, which is justly made on behalf of human rights—for example, the right to health, to home, to work, to family, to culture — is false and illusory if the right to life, the most basic and fundamental right and the condition for all other personal rights, is not defended with maximum determination." **Pope John Paul II, Christifideles Laici (1988), 38**

"It is impossible to further the common good without acknowledging and defending the right to life, upon which all the other inalienable rights of individuals are founded and from which they develop. A society lacks solid foundations when, on the one hand, it asserts values such as the dignity of the person, justice and peace, but then, on the other hand, radically acts to the contrary by allowing or tolerating a variety of ways in which human life is devalued and violated, especially where it is weak or marginalized. Only respect for life can be the foundation and guarantee of the most precious and essential goods of society, such as democracy and peace." **Pope John Paul II, Evangelium vitae (1995), 101**

"The first right of the human person is his life. He has other goods and some are more precious, but this one is fundamental — the condition of all the others. Hence it must be protected above all others. It does not belong to society, nor does it belong to public authority in any

form to recognize this right for some and not for others: all discrimination is evil, whether it be founded on race, sex, color or religion. It is not recognition by another that constitutes this right. This right is antecedent to its recognition; it demands recognition and it is strictly unjust to refuse it." **Congregation for the Doctrine of the Faith, Declaration on Procured Abortion (1974), no.11 Resolution on Abortion (1989)**

"Among important issues involving the dignity of human life with which the Church is concerned, abortion necessarily plays a central role. Abortion, the direct killing of an innocent human being, is always gravely immoral (The Gospel of Life, no. 57); its victims are the most vulnerable and defenseless members of the human family. It is imperative that those who are called to serve the least among us give urgent attention and priority to this issue of justice." **USCCB Resolution on Abortion (1989)**

The general sense of despair and outrage over *Roe v Wade* has for long energized a significant portion of the American public, including a very large number of Roman Catholics as well as Evangelical and Pentecostal Protestants and others of good will.

The first March for Life, founded by Nellie Jane Gray (June 1924 –August 2012), a native of Big Spring, Texas, and later a Roman Catholic convert was held on January 22, 1974 on the West Steps of the Capitol, with an estimated 20,000 supporters in attendance. An employee of the federal government for twenty-eight years and a graduate of Georgetown University's School of Law, Ms. Gray had practiced law before the U.S. Supreme Court. After *Roe v Wade*, she retired from professional life and became a pro-life activist, beginning with the March for Life. Upon her death, Sean Cardinal O'Malley, Archbishop of Boston, hailed her as *"the Joan of Arc of the Gospel of Life."*

By the time of the 35th annual March for Life in 2008, statistics became available which revealed that the number of abortions performed in the United States had dropped to 1.2 million in 2005. This was the lowest level of abortions since 1976. Although this seemed like a victory, many march participants stressed that the figures were not a large enough decline. Many marchers said they would not stop protesting until abortions were illegal.

During the 2009 March for Life, the threat of passage by the 111th United States Congress of the Freedom of Choice Act—a bill that would "codify *Roe v. Wade*" by declaring a fundamental right to abortion and lifting many restrictions on abortion—served as a key rallying point, because pro-lifers worried that the legislation would eliminate certain abortion restrictions such as parental notification for minors and repeal the Partial-Birth Abortion Ban Act. The present controversy concerning provisions of the Affordable Care Act continues to energize participants in 2014. And so, the struggle continues.

Monday, January 20, 2014 was not unusually cold for Columbus Ohio. The Josephinum seminarians attended class as usual during the morning and early afternoon, and when three chartered buses of the American Interstate Bus company arrived shortly before 4:00 PM, the outside temperature was a relatively balmy 34°F. The buses would transport the Josephinum's contingent of over 135 seminarians, one of the largest contingents in the institution's history, to Washington DC for the 41st annual March for Life.

"This was my third March for Life. We had class on Monday morning and I had packed the night before so that I would be ready to leave at 4:00 PM. The bus ride went well, we watched two movies, conducted evening and night prayer on the bus as well as a rosary. No

one really slept on the way there. We got to the High School where we were staying and unloaded and settled down to get some sleep." **Timothy White— Second Year College—Lawrenceburg, KY—[Diocese of Lexington]**

After about an eight-hour hour ride to the Nation's Capital, the buses arrived in suburban Arlington Virginia, where the seminarians would remain overnight. About half of the seminarians stayed in the gymnasium at Bishop O'Connell High School on North Little Falls Road,while the remainder "camped out" at Our Lady of Lourdes Roman Catholic Parish on South 23rd Street nearby.

Weather conditions deteriorated markedly overnight, as a nor'easter made its way up the eastern seaboard. By dawn on Tuesday it was centered off Cape Henlopen, Delaware, and its impact was being felt from Richmond to Philadelphia. After a short night's rest, the seminarians arose about 6:30 AM, and after local devotions and breakfast were free to explore the city –where all governmental activity was suspended due to the storm – as best they could for several hours.

"Tuesday, we were allotted some touring time of D.C. The group I was with went to Union station, and then walked through the city. We saw the Lincoln Memorial, Vietnam Memorial, The Washington Monument, the White House, Supreme Court, Congress, Treasury Building and many other buildings. All the while it was snowing and blowing which made some things hard to see, and the cold didn't make anything better. Then we went back to the school and got changed into our cassocks to go to the Basilica vigil mass that night. That was awesome, being there with so many people, brother seminarians, priests, bishops and cardinals. And being able to process in the opening procession was amazing!" **[Timothy White]**

"I was eating by myself before the liturgy. I was eavesdropping on a conversation occurring at the table next to me. The two men kept mentioning key words as "philosophy studies" or "Pope Francis" or the "Jesuits" which attracted my attention. With the March for Life occurring there were many Catholics roaming around the city so I had the courage to kindly interrupt and ask where they were from. It turned out that the one man named Peter was a Scholastic of the Coptic Church doing his student teaching in California, though originally from somewhere in the Middle East. He came to D.C. as a field trip to show his students up close how the government works, but the March also allowed him more opportunity to teach and attend various functions such as the Mass for all attending Jesuits at a local church. His friend had been a philosophy student with Peter sometime earlier and had since become good friends with him. After I told Peter I went to the Josephinum, he said that he had heard good things about the seminary. I was surprised about his familiarity with the place. Seeing that someone from across the country knew of my school, it made me realize more about my identity as a representative in D.C. After more good conversation and promised prayers for each other, I continued on my way. Looking back on the experience I noticed how close the Universal Church can bring together two total strangers. Even among all our differences, there was a comfort and excitement in that conversation which I now realize to be the union we both had in Jesus Christ. This realization helped my overall bond with all the other marchers supporting a common goal." **Austin Windland — First Year College—Belpre OH —[Diocese of Steubenville]**

The seminarians made their way later that afternoon to participate in Holy Mass at the The Basilica of the National Shrine of the Immaculate Conception, the largest Roman Catholic church in North America. After vesting in the under-croft of the Basilica with hundreds of other seminarians and clergy, they processed in unison at 6:30pm to the Great Upper Church for the 2014 National

Prayer Vigil for Life which began with the Solemn Opening Mass. His Eminence, Cardinal Sean O'Malley, Chairman of the USCCB's Committee on Pro-Life Activities and Cardinal-Archbishop of Boston was the principal celebrant and homilist.

"The Tuesday before the March was our 'free day', and it snowed quite a bit. The rumor mill was just as efficient at my site as it is at the seminary: wrong information about the Metro rail being shut down passed among us. A friend and I went out anyway and found the rail intact; we went to the Air and Space Museum (he'd never been).

At the Air and Space museum, a few janitors engaged us in conversation; since we weren't planning on returning to our sleeping site before the March for Life Vigil Mass, we were wearing our cassocks, and these janitors took notice. We had a short, light-hearted conversation, and they offered to pray for us and asked for our prayers.

The Basilica Mass is always beautiful, chaotic, and bizarre all at once. The seminarians and priests assemble in the Crypt, being given instructions about where to stand and how quiet to be, which they then promptly ignore as they mingle with long-lost friends. As the Mass began this year, they lined us up into rows, and we waited in anticipation. Suddenly we were moving, then stopped, and some ad hoc choir members were squeezing past us, and then we were suddenly in the nave of the Basilica and processing into the Mass.

As usual, we were seated toward the back; I was thankful for the seat, as last year many of us were standing and kneeling on the marble itself." **Richard Childress—Second Year Pre-Theology— Nashville, Tn.—[Diocese of Nashville]**

"The best part for me this year was the vigil Mass at the Basilica of the Shrine of the Immaculate Conception. Aside from being with my

Josephinum brothers, I had the opportunity to reunite with old friends, some who are seminarians, from Franciscan University who are now based all over the country. It was a powerful experience processing in for Mass with hundreds of seminarians, deacons, and priests, so many bishops, and a few cardinals. It was a microcosm of the Universal Church!" **J. Michael Villanueva—First Year Theology—Anthem, AZ—[Diocese of Phoenix]**

"My most memorable moment this March for Life was during the procession at the Vigil Mass at the Basilica of the National Shrine of the Immaculate Conception. This is always an inspiring moment because of the vast number of people who have come to Mass and number of priests, seminarians, and bishops. As we were processing in, I was in the mid-to-back of the seminarian section. As we processed, I looked at the faces of the large amount of people who were there. Most of them had smiles on their faces. One lady at the front had her eyes close and tears streaming down her faces. These experiences remind me of the witness I am. Just my presence as a young man in a cassock and collar seeking to be a priest of Jesus Christ inspires people and draws them closer to Him. It gives them hope and humbles me. How blessed am I that the Lord would choose to use me to bring about salvation in the world!" **Rhodes Bolster— Third Year College—Nashville, TN— [Diocese of Nashville]**

The Josephinum seminarians returned to their temporary billets after the Mass, and prepared for the next morning's rally on the national Mall and the march to the Supreme Court.

Joining thousands of young people from across the United States and braving near-record low temperatures and Arctic-type wind chills, they first gathered in downtown Washington for another rally and Mass prior to the March itself.

"We can help the world understand that no one is an accident, all have a purpose and are loved because each person has the face of Jesus Christ," Father Michael Paris, a priest of the archdiocese told more than 10,000 youth who gathered for the Mass for Life at the Verizon Center.

The Mass was celebrated by Cardinal Donald W. Wuerl of Washington. Concelebrants included several bishops, including Washington Auxiliary Bishop Martin D. Holley, and more than 160 priests.

"I believe God wants to use us to end abortion. … By helping the world see that God has a plan for each life, that everyone is loved by God," Father Paris continued. *"If people believed that, they would never think that killing a child could be an option…Abortion cannot stand if each person believes this."*

At the conclusion of the Mass, the seminarians joined the other participants as they braved the frigid temperatures and walked the seven blocks to their assigned position on the Mall, just outside the doors of the Natural History Museum at 10th St. & Constitution Avenue, NW.

"Another aspect of the March for Life is summed up nicely in the often quoted saying regarding the event that, 'every Catholic you have ever known will be there.' Considering this quote more humorous cliche than reality I would throw it around as a joke whenever I bumped into an old friend of acquaintance. This year however I became a believer. Following my junior year of college I took a year off to serve overseas as a lay missionary. I met a fellow missionary from Scotland around my age and we became fast friends over the next year. As life caught up to us both we lost contact; I entered the busy life that is seminary and he became a novice for the Franciscan Friars of the Renewal. At the youth Mass at the Verizon Center I was walking among the youth

group I had traveled with and lo behold there he was, full habit and bearded! We saw each other simultaneously, dropped our conversations, ran full speed at each other, and embraced. There are not really words to describe the providential happening when two good brothers in Christ reunite after a period of years. With so many people around our reunion drew a crowd as this young friar and seminarian in cassock and collar rejoiced in each others' presence. No one seemed fazed by the event though, just pleased, like this was natural. At the March for Life every Catholic you have ever known is in fact there." [Daniel Swartz]

Others, unfortunately, had less luck in meeting up with old friends or associates:

"The March for Life reflects the unity of the Church from across the nation. This trip was my sixth March for Life. When I first started to go in high school, it seemed like a vacation, but every year since, it becomes progressively religious.

One thing that aids (rather than detracts from the spirit of the protestors) are the rugged conditions. During the week of the march, Washington D.C. fills up fast and so in high school we always stayed at the most run-down motel available, and once I got into seminary, I went even lower - to a concrete Franciscan basement! The last two years we moved to a hallway/auditorium at Bishop O' Connell high school, which sounds less pleasant, but they at least had carpet.

This year over the two days, I spent a considerable amount of time trying to find friends that I've met from across the country. In the search, I felt empathetic to any grandparents who swear they walked uphill both ways to school in four inches of snow, etc. In past years, I was able to meet up with friends from New York, Ohio, West Virginia and Indiana, but this year I failed in all attempts to connect with old friends.

146

After bracing against the first round of Snowmaggaedon, I saw I had about four hours to meet up with Father Michael Hennigan (alumni of the Josephinum) and my high school. I was texting my sister and Father Michael in order to find their lodgings, which coincidentally were within two miles of Bishop O' Connell high school. From the Mall to East Falls Church Metro station, was about an hour. On the bus, I found out my high school was staying at a Comfort Inn somewhere in the area. I had my cassock, surplice, black pants, black socks and shoes in my backpack and so figured it would not be an issue to slip in a couple visits before the Mass at the Basilica later that night. Snowmaggaedon round-two began falling, salt trucks were flying, salt was turning 4-6 inches of snow into puddles I tried jumping over. I kept going, pulled out my rosary and started to pray (subtlety though). I finally saw a Comfort Inn, and after waiting for a few traffic lights, I ran in the front door, pulled off my hat and asked the front desk, "Is there a high school staying here by any chance?" "Uhm, no?" "Hmmm, thank you!" With about three hours left, I calculated again. An hour and a half to get to the Basilica - 45 minute walk, hour bus ride. I walk faster than the average person, so I knew I could cut that time down. I hope Father Hennigan isn't waiting on me though! "**Joey Collopy—Fourth Year College—Ft.Thomas, Ky.—[Diocese of Covington]**"

Air temperature at noon at the reporting station at Andrews AFB nearby registered 11F. (-11.7C) with brisk Northwest winds gusting to 16 MPH, making the wind chill on Constitution Avenue -6F according to the National Weather Service. Nevertheless, and with crunchy snow underfoot, a crowd estimated at 200,000 participants and spanning several blocks huddled on the National Mall to hear speakers such as Representative Eric Cantor of Virginia, the Republican House majority leader, before marching past the Capitol to the Supreme Court. At a gathering earlier, speakers included Jason Jones, the filmmaker behind the movie "Bella," about a waitress who chooses not to have an abortion when she unexpectedly becomes pregnant.

Organizers had made adoption the theme of this year's event and invited an evangelical pastor to speak to the mostly Roman Catholic crowd. The pastor, James Dobson, appeared with his adopted son to close out the ceremony.

"Adoption is a heroic decision for pregnant mothers who find themselves in a difficult situation," said Jeanne Monahan, the current president of March for Life, *"We want to eliminate the stigma of adoption and encourage women to pursue this noble option."* Rick Santorum, the Republican former senator from Pennsylvania and a 2012 presidential candidate, said the movement had become one "of love, not of judgment."

The march drew support from Pope Francis himself. *"I join the March for Life in Washington with my prayers. May God help us respect all life, especially the most vulnerable."*

Regrettably, as he has done in previous years, President Obama in a press release on Wednesday, committed to abide by the Roe v. Wade decision's "guiding principle: that every woman should be able to make her own choices about her body and her health. *"We reaffirm our steadfast commitment to protecting a woman's access to safe, affordable health care and her constitutional right to privacy, including the right to reproductive freedom,"* he said.

The participants, some from as far away as the West Coast and Canada, and clad in thick layers of clothing, again carried signs proclaiming "I Stand For Life" and "We Are The Pro-Life Generation" as the orderly and peaceful marchers processed slowly from the Mall to the steps of the Supreme Court.

The Josephinum seminarians had listened attentively to the various speakers and waited their turn to join the line of march to the steps of the Supreme Court for additional prayer. Because of the size of the crowd that they did not arrive at the Supreme Court building until nearly 2:30 PM.

"The March itself seemed shorter this year, possibly because our group was more organized than last year (and so there was so much less stress). I met up with an old friend living in Georgia who took me out to lunch, and from there we went to the designated 'Josephinum spot' in front of the Natural History Museum; my friend marched with us, and we began praying the Rosary. Being with all my brothers, praying, was awesome. Whoever was leading whichever prayer prayed through a megaphone, and at one point the leader said, 'Josephinum, move toward the middle. We're going to try to outrun the IPF [International Pro-Life Federation]'. This particular group always brings drums and is gloriously noisy, but making our prayers difficult when we end up near them. Despite it being only 11F or so, not including wind-chill, when we began marching it was not that cold; I suspect the thousands of bodies and the sun helped (it was much better than that morning, when the wind and a sand-consistency snow cut through my scarf). Then it was suddenly over, surprisingly. We didn't see any protesters, and everywhere groups were celebrating, chanting, and praying. We took our picture, and then I (and a few brothers) hot-footed it to a Metro station before it shut down." [Richard Childress]

We would be seriously remiss, however, if we didn't recount the story of the extraordinary efforts of one Josephinum seminarian to participate in the March for Life:

"I have been on several Marches for Life over the years but this year was the most challenging march yet. It all started while I was playing

basketball about two weeks before the March, when I suffered a serious sprain to my ankle. As I lay writhing in pain with a crowd of seminarians leaning over me, I knew my chances of going on the March had plummeted. The sprain was so serious that I had to be pushed in a wheel chair to the nurse's office. I thought about how much I loved going on the March for Life. You see, I consider it a pleasant misery, sort of like camping. You plan and get excited and think you are going to have a stupendous time. When you are actually camping all you can do is think about how miserable you are, but lo and behold, not long after returning you are already thinking about how much fun you will have next time.

It is the same for the March for Life. I look forward to it, hate it when I am there, and cannot wait to go the next time. But there was an obstacle to going this year. If I went on crutches, I ran the risk of slipping on some long flight of icy stairs and injuring myself further. If I brought a wheel chair, someone would have to push me everywhere. If I decided not to use either, my ankle would certainly get worse. The first full day on crutches I knew what a pain navigating stairs was; the Josephinum is a great maze of stairwells. By the end of an average day I could barely climb to my room on the second story. I decided to go to the doctor for an x-ray. I was relieved to hear that the x-rays only showed old ankle fractures and thus my injury was only a serious sprain. But that did not relieve me of the crutches. With the march only two days away, eight days after I got my injury, I fully expected not to go to the March. But it was not personal indecision stopping me now, rather it was my kind formation adviser who did not want to see me crack my skull open on the ice. If he did not stop me, I was determined to go regardless of the suffering I might incur. However, I resolved that I would obey the wisdom of my formation adviser, regardless of my will. One way or the other, I would suffer for Christ, the unborn babies, and the adult victims of abortion: if I could not go, I would grow in obedience offering up missing my favorite event of the year; if I could go, I

*would suffer more that I ever had on the March. I talked to my forma-
tion adviser twice about the situation. He asked what the weather was
going to be. "4-6 inches of snow and about 12 degrees" I said.*

*The day before the March God's will for me was revealed: I got an
email permitting me to go. Before I knew it, I was on the bus. The next
morning I arose from the concrete floor (somehow the concrete feels softer
every year, maybe my nerve endings are getting destroyed). I set out
with a group of seminarian friends to hit some museums before the vigil
Mass at the National Shrine. The March was the next day. Many
museums had closed at the threat of now 6-8 inches of snow which was
expected in the afternoon. Nevertheless my group toured three museums
that day.*

*I never would have made it the first day if it had not been for the help
of my seminarian friends. Somehow I managed to hobble along with the
other seminarians in the opening procession. We were exhilarated to be
there.*

*The next day we arrived in the Mall for the March. The march started
and the seminarians of the Josephinum prayed and sang the whole way.
I had missed several meals and became exhausted. I fought my way
through the crowds until we reached Capital Hill. My energy was gone,
I was cold, injured, and dehydrated. At the top of the hill I suddenly
met my mom and my sister. I think I know a bit what Christ felt
like on Calvary now. The March ended but we still had to get back. I
became dizzy and nearly collapsed twice. My friends helped me on the
last few blocks of the journey. I could no longer keep up with the group
but Nick Ginnetti gave me a cookie. He has no idea how helpful that
cookie was.*

*My friends, my family, my God pulled me through. I never realized so
many people loved me so much. Maybe our suffering saved some souls*

151

but I learned this: we only know what we suffer." **Zach Brown—Third Year College—Attica, Ohio—[Diocese of Toledo]**

At the conclusion of the March the Josephinum seminarians travel via the DC Metro lines back to their temporary billets, and after a brief warm-up, re-boarded their buses for the journey back to the Josephinum, arriving well after midnight. After a short night's rest back at the Josephinum, they were ready for their 8:30 AM classes the following morning.

POSTSCRIPT:

When Brothers Dwell Together

The ink-stained wretch who had written these words stepped from the shadows, where he had lurked these many months eavesdropping on the conversations and recollections of the Josephinum's seminarians. The annual commencement ceremonies were completed and the deacon class had return to their home dioceses for priestly ordination. Others had departed for mission trips to South America and beyond; still others would return to the summer embrace of family and friends. For a few, particularly those making the transition from collegiate to theological studies, this had been their last semester at the Josephinum, and depending on their own diocese's practices, next semester would find them in another seminary. And some would complete their discernment experience and pursue other life goals, outside the clerical state.

Unfortunately, all the brothers who dwelt together would not likely be in the same place at the same time ever again. Even for reunions, there is always someone who can't make it back, and as the years roll on, one or two may have been promoted by death from the Church Militant to the Church Triumphant. Life in the seminary is a collection of snapshots: life at the Josephinum will never be exactly the same again.

153

The Josephinum will persevere, of course. One hundred twenty-five years of history, after all, does presume some staying power. And as the seminarians leave for the summer, filling dumpsters and other receptacles with the detritus of yet another school year, the hard-working facilities staff turn again to their the annual maintenance routines which will preserve this "House which Joseph Built" for generations yet unborn.

It is always sad for the staff to say goodbye to students at year's end. It can even be so for those superannuated staff unlikely to be mistaken for one of the brothers—more likely as a favorite uncle or grandfather perhaps—but not likely as a seminarian. It's a youngster's game, this.

The writer reflected on all this as he slowly shuttled the contents of his office to his car. Time, and the lingering effects of a recent stroke had slowed his steps, but as he trundled to the parking lot, he recalled other summers a half-century past, when he too had bade farewell to seminary classmates as he and they rushed to pile books, clothes and the occasional typewriter or eight-track player into the trunks of taxis waiting patiently to transport them to airport or railway station.

For as one approaches the proverbial three-score-and-ten, it's amazing how easy it becomes to conjure up memories of distant times; even if just as frequently it becomes necessary to enlist the services of the grandkids to help locate a missing wallet or TV-remote. The writer pondered this disturbing gift of the Confusing Angel as he stopped to catch his breath in the tree-lined drive leading away from the Josephinum.

He could recall with almost perfect clarity that September Sunday of fifty years past, when his family deposited him on the steps of

St. Peter's Seminary (Paulist Fathers) in Baltimore. The rector's letter said to arrive no later than three PM; but Pop, who was about as likely to be caught reading *Pravda* as caught reading a road map, took a wrong turn in the inner city of Baltimore and we—mom, my sister, two brothers and I, were treated to an extensive excursion through neighborhoods which years later became the backdrop for *Homicide-Life on the Street,* and HBO's *The Wire.* The glove box of that '61 Plymouth Station Wagon was chock full of road maps, as was the custom in those pre-GPS times, but Pop discouraged us from disturbing them, lest we fail to master the intricate origami of refolding them to fit back in their accustomed place. And stopping to ask directions was a unthinkable confession of inadequacy.

The sounds of Gregorian chant — I recall *Ubi Caritas* wafting through the open windows of the chapel —greeted us as we pulled up shortly before five o'clock. Chagrined, excited, but scared out of my wits at the thought of my first night away from home, I searched in vain for anyone — the rector, the procurator, the Ghost of Christmas past, anyone — to tell me what to do next. Pop and the rest of the clan, anxious to get home to Philadelphia before nightfall, began piling suitcases full of my worldly possessions — black trousers, black overcoat, black socks, black-everything, and neatly stenciled too— on the front sidewalk.

"Ubi caritas et amor, deus ibi est" – Where charity and love prevail, God is ever found. Just as at the Josephinum, as the liturgy ended upperclassman pitched in willingly, and soon had thing well in hand. My mom and sister pronounced my room fit for human habitation, although there were a few snide comments about its likely condition after I'd occupied it for a while. We said goodbye: Mom cried a little, and I went to supper. I never did learn what misadventures greeted them on the return trip through the uncharted wilds of Maryland and Delaware.

After the meal we newly-minted seminarians remained in the refectory to meet key members of the faculty. The Rector, Father William Manning CSP, and Father Ralph Carpenter CSP, his Procurator, laid out a basic overview of the discernment and formation processes. Father Vinnie McKiernan CSP, a recently ordained Paulist whose years of theological education did little to attenuate his broad New York accent, was appointed to look after the new guys who would lodge on the third floor. And Father Austin Malone CSP, whom I came to admire and to love as perhaps the wisest and most saintly man I've ever known, was introduced as our spiritual adviser. My mind reeling from the events of the day, I made a bee-line to my new room after evening prayer, being certain to observe the *"Magnum Silentium"* which would prevail till the completion of morning Mass.

Now, you must recall that in those pre-Vatican II days, seminary life was more like the Josephinum described in Chapter Two than seminary life today. Even in a community as markedly progressive as the Paulist Fathers (and the first canard I learned at St. Peter's was that CSP actually stood for "Congregation of Semi-Protestants!") standards had to be met, and St. Charles Borromeo, great reformer of sixteenth century seminaries would not have been displeased had he wandered by for dinner. Which, like most meals, was consumed in silence, accompanied only by a timid seminarian reading from the lives of the saints.

This is not to say the spirit was unwilling. Indeed our spirits *were* willing, even though our flesh was weak. These were heady times remember; the election of JFK and the elevation of Pope John XXIII brought winds of change sweeping through church and state alike. Many of our peer-leaders were involved with the Catholic Worker Movement of Dorothy Day and Peter Maurin [Note to any seminary officials who might be reading this: If you think that you can readily counteract the impact of peer pressure on your seminarians, think again.] And some of the more radical among us were even influenced by the worker-priest movement of Father Jacques Loew on the docks of Marseilles.

A story, perhaps apocryphal, remains with me still. Two seminarians approaching ordination were overheard discussing their hopes regarding first assignments. "Where do you want to go, Bill? A nice city parish or somewhere out in the country?" "I was thinking more of Bethlehem Steel, to tell the truth, Jim!" While these days I notice a distinct affection for traditionalism and even a faint whiff of clericalism, especially among the younger seminarians; we were all young iconoclasts, and Liberation Theology was our rallying cry back then. There's a Yiddish proverb — "*Velkh der Zeyde vilst keyn fargesn, der kind vilst keyn gedenken*"—"What the grandfather longs to forget, the child wishes to remember." Perhaps it has always been so.

As the months and years rolled by, the inevitable attrition began to take its toll. We'd awake, and Joe or Jim or Tom would be gone, never to be contacted or even to be spoken of again. The rules were clear: seminarians who left could not return, not even to visit, and correspondence or even contact outside the seminary were not permitted. Even casual reference in class or amongst the remaining seminarians was strongly discouraged.

It's not that I was an ideal, nor even a particularly zealous member of the community. I recall a series of rather awkward conversations, first with Father Malone and later with the Rector, who pointed out that my penchant for sneaking out to date student nurses at Bon Secours Hospital downtown was not particularly career enhancing in the celibate world of the Missionary Society of Saint Paul the Apostle. The last conversation took place in the Rector's study one snowy winter's evening several years later when he suggested that I go home for a while to reconsider my vocation at my leisure and stop disturbing the brothers by the rattling of the fire escape during my night time excursions. He reached into a desk drawer and offered me thirty dollars for the train fare. I did resist the urge to ask for pieces of silver, thank God.

I recount all this now with no sense of pride in my immaturity, nor any animus to those to whose care I was entrusted. I went off, fought as a Navy Seabee in Vietnam, married a [former] student nurse, and spent over thirty years in the defense intelligence community and the telecommunications industry. But my years with the Paulists had become part of me, and I've cherished them ever since.

A few years ago, while serving as the Josephinum's Vice President for Strategic Planning and Extension Services, at the Rector's request I undertook a study of the attrition rates of the Josephinum compared to the other forty-six seminaries in the United States. It was satisfying to learn that our "through-put" (students, who, within ten years after entering as a collegian were ordained as priests) was significantly above the twenty-three percent which prevailed nationwide. More satisfying still were discussions with many who returned for our summer reunions, priests and laymen alike. Their experiences mirrored mine and those of my classmates: on the whole they went on to successful lives as educators, businessmen or professionals in many disciplines.

I'd kept track of many of my old friends over the years as well: Tony became a successful insurance professional in California; Paul became a lawyer in Canada, and later took silk as Queen's Counsel in his native Prince Edward Island; Kevin became one of New York City's finest and retired as a Borough Commander. At least two others became practicing psychologists, and one a respected Lutheran pastor in upstate New York. And yet another (more liturgically minded than most), became, at least for a time, a Hare Krishna devotee in San Francisco. We think it may have been the saffron robes and incense which attracted him.

So we've come now full circle from where we've begun. Recall these words from our first chapter: *"Discernment is all about developing a relationship with God so that we can see our life as God sees it, and accept the plan which the Creator has in store for us. [It] helps us become more aware of what's going on in our daily life, to be more sensitive to our deeper desires and hopes, as well as our reactions or responses to the world around us."*

No one has a vocation to the *seminary*. It's just a train ride, long and tedious as it might seem, from where we are to where we perceive God wants us to go. We all buy a ticket for the full ride, but some may find it more appropriate to alight at a station along the way. We cross the platform and hop aboard a train toward another destination. And that's discernment too.

There have been many evolutions in priestly education in the past half century. Certainly, one has been abandonment of the attitude that leaving the seminary is an embarrassment or a personal failure. There need be no shame attached to the seminarian who heeds the still small voice which says "it's time to go". Your bishop will understand – he's seen it all before. Your mom may be devastated, but she'll get over it; and once the dust settles, you'll feel better about the decision too. I've never met a former seminarian who doesn't look back on his years in seminary without a sense of pride in having given it a shot, and great fondness for the place which helped to form him into the person whom he is today.

Thank you to all the fine young men who contributed with such candor and good humor to this story. May each of you soon arrive at that special moment when you lie prone on the cathedral floor in the presence of your prelate, family and those new brothers with whom you'll serve the faithful of your diocese or community. And may the Holy Spirit continue to guide you and direct your footsteps, whatever path you may take, and may you all be fulfilled and sanctified along the road ahead.

How good and how pleasant it is,
when brothers dwell together as one!
Like fine oil on the head
running down upon the beard.
Upon the beard of Aaron,
upon the collar of his robe.

God bless you all, my brothers, and may the peace of the Lord be with you always.

REFERENCES:

Chapter One: Discerning Your Vocation

Narrative derived from:Committee on Priestly Formation of the United States Conference of Catholic Bishops (USCCB). (2005). The program of priestly formation. (5TH ed.,pages 15-28, paragraphs 32-67). Washington D.C.: United States Conference of Catholic Bishops (USCCB). DOI: www.usccb.org

We are grateful for permission to quote these current Josephinum seminarians in this Chapter:

Jesse Garza, Third Year Theology, Mission, TX, [Diocese of Brownsville]

Michael Hartge, Third Year Theology, Reynoldsburg, OH, [Diocese of Columbus]

J. Michael Villanueva, First Year Theology, Anthem, AZ, [Diocese of Phoenix]

Edward Shikina, Fourth Year Pre-Theology, Columbus, OH, [Diocese of Columbus]

Brett Garland, Second Year Pre-Theology, Washington CH,Ohio, [Diocese of Columbus]

Estevan Wetzel, Fourth Year College, Phoenix, AZ, [Diocese of Phoenix]

Zach Brown, Third Year College, Attica, Ohio, [Diocese of Toledo]

Chapter Two: The House that Joseph Built

Narrative derived from:

FICK, REVEREND MONSIGNOR LEONARD J.(1988). The Jessing Legacy 1888-1988 A Centennial History Of The Pontifical College Josephinum. (pp. 20-24, pp. 65-67). Columbus, Ohio: KAIROS BOOKS. DOI: www.pcj.edu

COONEY, REVEREND MONSIGNOR ROGER P. (1999). The Spirit Of John Joseph Jessing: Priest, Orphan's Friend, Visionary. (pp. 29-52). Columbus Ohio: The Pontifical College Josephinium (privately printed). DOI: www.pcj.edu

MATTINGLY, H. E. (1979).Frank A. Ludewig, Architect. (Vol. V, pp. 411-413). COLUMBUS, OHIO: BULLETIN OF THE CATHOLIC RECORDS SOCIETY. DOI: WWW.DIOCCOL.ORG

KLEINZ, J. P. (1985). John Joseph Jessing. (Vol. X, pp. 25-31). COLUMBUS, OHIO: BULLETIN OF THE CATHOLIC RECORDS SOCIETY. DOI: WWW.DIOCCOL.ORG

RIPPLEY, L. J. (1999). The Columbus Germans. INDIANAPOLIS, IN: Max Kade German-American Center & Indiana German Heritage Society,. ISBN 1880788128, 9781880788127, 52 pages

We are grateful for permission to quote these current Josephinum seminarians in this Chapter:

Dean Carson, First Year Theology, Louisville, OH, [Diocese of Columbus] Richard Childress, Second Year Pre-Theology, Nashville,Tn., [Diocese of Nashville]

REFERENCES:

Brian Aerts, First Year Pre-Theology, San Antonio, NM, [Diocese of Santa Fe]

Mitchel Roman, First Year Pre-Theology, Empire MI [Diocese of Gaylord]

Gordon Mott, First Year Pre-Theology, Columbus Ohio, [Diocese of Columbus]

Estevan Wetzel, Fourth Year College, Phoenix, AZ, [Diocese of Phoenix]

Joey Collopy, Fourth Year College, Ft.Thomas, Ky., [Diocese of Covington]

Zach Brown, Third Year College, Attica, Ohio, [Diocese of Toledo]

Blaise Radel, Second Year College, Arlington,Va, [Diocese of Arlington]

<u>Chapter Three: Life In Community</u>

Narrative derived from:Committee on Priestly Formation of the United States Conference of Catholic Bishops (USCCB). (2005). The program of priestly formation. (5TH ed, Pages 85-89, paragraphs 258-271). Washington D.C.: United States Conference of Catholic Bishops (USCCB). DOI: www.usccb.org

We are grateful for permission to quote these current Josephinum seminarians in this Chapter:

Jesse Garza, Third Year Theology, Mission, TX, [Diocese of Brownsville]

Daniel Swartz, Second Year Theology, Columbus Ohio, [Diocese of Columbus]

Dean Carson, First Year Theology, Louisville, OH, [Diocese of Columbus]

J. Michael Villanueva, First Year Theology, Anthem, AZ, [Diocese of Phoenix]

Richard Childress, Second Year Pre-Theology, Nashville,Tn., [Diocese of Nashville]

Brett Garland, Second Year Pre-Theology, Washington CH,Ohio, [Diocese of Columbus]

Brian Aerts, First Year Pre-Theology, San Antonio, NM, [Diocese of Santa Fe]

Mitchel Roman, First Year Pre-Theology, Empire MI [Diocese of Gaylord]
Estevan Wetzel, Fourth Year College, Phoenix, AZ, [Diocese of Phoenix]

Chapter Four: On Becoming More Authentically Human

Narrative derived from:Committee on Priestly Formation of the United States Conference of Catholic Bishops (USCCB). (2005). The program of priestly formation. (5TH ed. Pages 29-41, paragraphs 74-105). Washington D.C.: United States Conference of Catholic Bishops (USCCB). DOI: www.usccb.org

We are grateful for permission to quote these current Josephinum seminarians in this Chapter:

Jesse Garza, Third Year Theology, Mission, TX, [Diocese of Brownsville]
Michael Hartge, Third Year Theology, Reynoldsburg, OH, [Diocese of Columbus]
Joseph Dalheim, Second Year Theology, Temple, TX [Diocese of Austin}
Dean Carson, First Year Theology, Louisville, OH, [Diocese of Columbus]
J. Michael Villanueva, First Year Theology, Anthem, AZ, [Diocese of Phoenix]
Craig Osburn, Second Year Pre-Theology, Carol Stream. Il, [Diocese of Joliet]
Gordon Mott, First Year Pre-Theology, Columbus Ohio, [Diocese of Columbus]
Estevan Wetzel, Fourth Year College, Phoenix, AZ, [Diocese of Phoenix]

Chapter Five: Spiritual Formation For Priesthood

Narrative derived from:Committee on Priestly Formation of the United States Conference of Catholic Bishops (USCCB). (2005). The program of priestly formation. (5TH ed.,Pages 42-52. paragraphs 106-135). Washington D.C.: United States Conference of Catholic Bishops (USCCB). DOI: www. usccb.org

We are grateful for permission to quote these current Josephinum seminarians in this Chapter:

Michael Hartge, Third Year Theology, Reynoldsburg, OH, [Diocese of Columbus]

Joshua Bartlett, Third Year Theology, Liberty. MO, [Diocese of KC/St. Joseph]

Tom Gardner, Third Year Theology, Bexley, OH, [Diocese of Columbus]

Joseph Dalheim, Second Year Theology, Temple, TX [Diocese of Austin]

J. Michael Villanueva, First Year Theology, Anthem, AZ, [Diocese of Phoenix]

Craig Osburn, Second Year Pre-Theology, Carol Stream. Il, [Diocese of Joliet]

Mitchel Roman, First Year Pre-Theology, Empire MI [Diocese of Gaylord]

Estevan Wetzel, Fourth Year College, Phoenix, AZ, [Diocese of Phoenix]

Zach Brown, Third Year College, Attica, Ohio, [Diocese of Toledo]

Joseph Finke, Third Year College, Ft. Wright, Ky., [Diocese of Covington]

Blaise Radel, Second Year College, Arlington,Va, [Diocese of Arlington]

Chapter Six: A Sound Mind in a Sound Body

Narrative derived from:Committee on Priestly Formation of the United States Conference of Catholic Bishops (USCCB). (2005). The program of priestly formation. (5TH ed Pages53-76, paragraphs 136- 235). Washington D.C.: United States Conference of Catholic Bishops (USCCB). DOI: www.usccb.org

We are grateful for permission to quote these current Josephinum seminarians in this Chapter:

Michael Hartge, Third Year Theology, Reynoldsburg, OH, [Diocese of Columbus]

Joseph Dalheim, Second Year Theology, Temple, TX [Diocese of Austin]

J. Michael Villanueva, First Year Theology, Anthem, AZ, [Diocese of Phoenix]

Chris Bond, First Year Theology, Cornelius, NC, [Diocese of Charlotte]

Mitchel Roman, First Year Pre-Theology, Empire MI [Diocese of Gaylord]

Michael Carlson, First Year Pre-Theology, Charlotte NC, [Diocese of Charlotte]

Will Nyce, First Year Pre-Theology, Vienna, VA, [Diocese of Arlington]

Vinhson Nguyen, Fourth Year College, Chandler AZ, [Diocese of Phoenix]

Joseph Finke, Third Year College, Ft. Wright, Ky., [Diocese of Covington]

Blaise Radel, Second Year College, Arlington,Va, [Diocese of Arlington]

Chapter Seven: Formation For Effective Ministry

Narrative derived from:Committee on Priestly Formation of the United States Conference of Catholic Bishops (USCCB). (2005). The program of priestly formation. (5TH ed., Pages 236- 257 paragraphs 76-81). Washington D.C.: United States Conference of Catholic Bishops (USCCB). DOI: www.usccb.org

We are grateful for permission to quote these current Josephinum seminarians in this Chapter:

Michael Hartge, Third Year Theology, Reynoldsburg, OH, [Diocese of Columbus]

Brian Seiler, Third Year Theology, Alexandria, LA, [Diocese of Alexandria]

Joseph Dalheim, Second Year Theology, Temple, TX [Diocese of Austin]

Daniel Swartz, Second Year Theology, Columbus Ohio, [Diocese of Columbus]

J. Michael Villanueva, First Year Theology, Anthem, AZ, [Diocese of Phoenix]

Josh Altonji, First Year Theology, Huntsville, AL, [Diocese of Birmingham]

Edward Shikina, Fourth Year, Pre-Theology, Columbus Ohio, [Diocese of Columbus]

REFERENCES:

Richard Childress, Second Year Pre-Theology, Nashville,Tn., [Diocese of Nashville]

Timothy Davis, Second Year Pre-Theology, Chadwick IL, [Diocese of Santa Fe]

Christopher Hamilton, Second Year Pre-Theology, Gastonia NC, [Diocese of Charlotte]

Will Nyce, First Year Pre-Theology, Vienna, VA – [Diocese of Arlington]

Thomas Herge, -First Year Pre-Theology, Columbus Ohio, [Diocese of Columbus]

Joey Collopy, Fourth Year College, Ft.Thomas, Ky., [Diocese of Covington]

David Freundl, First Year College –Traverse City MI, [Diocese of Gaylord]

Daniel Rice, First Year College, Chantilly,Va, [Diocese of Arlington]

Chapter Eight: The March For Life In Washington

Narrative derived from:

JOHN PAUL II, P. *(1988). Christifideles laici (1988), no. 38. Retrieved from http://www.vatican.va/holy_father/john_paul_ii/apost_exhortations/documents/hf_jp-ii_exh_30121988_christifideles-laici_en.html January, 2014*

JOHN PAUL II, P. *(1995). Evangelium vitae (1995), no. 101. Retrieved from http://www.vatican.va/holy_father/john_paul_ii/encyclicals/documents/hf_jp-ii_enc_25031995_evangelium-vitae_en.html January, 2014*

Congregation for the Doctrine of the Faith. *(1974). Declaration on procured abortion (1974), no.11 resolution on abortion (1989). Retrieved from http://www.vatican.va/roman_curia/congregations/cfaith/documents/rc_con_cfaith_doc_19741118_declaration-abortion_en.html January, 2014*

USCCB (1989). Resolution on abortion. *Retrieved from http://www.vatican.va/roman_curia/congregations/cfaith/documents/rc_con_cfaith_doc_19741118_declaration-abortion_en.html January, 2014*

PARKER, A. (JANUARY, 2014).2014 March For Life. Retrieved from http://topics.nytimes.com/top/reference/timestopics/people/p/ashley_parker/index.html January, 2014

SOUTHALL, A. (JANUARY 25,2014). march On Washington. Retrieved from http://thelede.blogs.nytimes.com/author/ashley-southall/2 January, 2014

MARCH FOR LIFEE COMMTTEE. (JANUARY 2104).Event details updated. Retrieved from http://marchforlife.org/march-with-us/details January, 2014

We are grateful for permission to quote these current Josephinum seminarians in this Chapter:

Joshua Bartlett, Third Year Theology, Liberty. MO, [Diocese of KC/St. Joseph]
Austin Windland, First Year College, Belpre OH, [Diocese of Steubenville]
Daniel Swartz, Second Year Theology, Columbus Ohio, [Diocese of Columbus]
J. Michael Villanueva, First Year Theology, Anthem, AZ, [Diocese of Phoenix]
Richard Childress, Second Year Pre-Theology, Nashville,Tn., [Diocese of Nashville]
Brian Aerts, First Year Pre-Theology, San Antonio, NM, [Diocese of Santa Fe]
Joey Collopy, Fourth Year College, Ft.Thomas, Ky., [Diocese of Covington]
Zach Brown, Third Year College, Attica, Ohio, [Diocese of Toledo]
Rhodes Bolster, Third Year College, Nashville, TN, [Diocese of Nashville]
Timothy White, Second Year College, Lawrenceburg, KY, [Diocese of Lexington]

ACKNOWLEDGMENTS

Although writing has been described as the loneliest of professions, no book is solely the work of the author listed on the cover. I am grateful for the collaboration and expertise of the seminarians, faculty and staff of the Pontifical College Josephinum who with great enthusiasm and good humor facilitated this project:

Special thanks are due to the thirty-seven seminarians quoted in this volume, and to others who provided additional insight and supported the project through their prayers, and;

Ms. Carolyn DiNovo, Director of Communications, who served as the primary editor of this volume. It is said that no man is a hero to his valet; neither is an author to his editor, especially an author with as tentative a grasp of the rule of punctuation as I. Thanks, Carolyn!

Ms Tracy Becker, herself a published author, who took charge of the routing and control of legal release forms, permissions and the myriad review manuscripts involved and whose ever-helpful and cheerful demeanor has brightened the Josephinum for many years.

Rev. Louis V. Isiello, OFM, PhD; Rev. Walter Oxley, STD and Rev. John F. Heisler MA, who kindly reviewed the manuscript and prevented me from wandering into "heresies and schisms you can commit yourself", which sometimes happens when I am writing above my level of competence.

Peter G. Veracka, Associate Professor of Theology and Director of Library Services, who for thirty-eight years has served as the living memory of the Josephinum, and whose ability to ferret out even the most obscure facts about the institution is truly astounding. It's in the footnotes, Peter!

Dr. Anne K. Dellinger formerly of Mount Saint Paul's College. A friend and colleague for over forty years, now retired to rural Virginia, Dr. Annie conducted valuable research including countless hours spent researching the annual March for Life, in which she has participated for many years. She is the only person I know who has been arrested during peaceful protests at both the Pentagon and the Supreme Court. Go get 'em, Dr. Annie!

ABOUT THE AUTHOR:

J.F. (Jack) Leahy *completed his undergraduate education at St. Peter's College, the Paulist Father's seminary in Baltimore. Upon leaving St. Peter's, he enlisted in the United States Navy, fighting as a Navy Seabee in Vietnam in 1969-70. After completing his graduate education at Abilene Christian University in Texas, he spent over thirty years in the defense intelligence community and telecommunications industry. Retiring in 2001, he became an adjunct professor at Franklin University in Ohio, and in 2006 was invited to develop the first distance learning programs for the permanent diaconate at the Josephinum. He retired as Vice President for Strategic Planning and Extension Services in 2011.*

OTHER BOOKS BY MR LEAHY:

Come From Away: The Plot to Assassinate Churchill – 1941
(Naval Writers Group, Annapolis MD, 2013) ISBN-13: 978-0615669625

Lost at Sea–An Enlisted Woman's Journey *(with Rebecca Anne Freeman). (Naval Writers Group, Annapolis MD, 2005) ISBN-13: 978-1595260956*

The Chief Petty Officer's Guide. *(With John Hagan) (Naval Institute Press, Annapolis, Maryland,2004). ISBN-13: 978-1591144595*

Ask The Chief – Backbone of the Navy *(Naval Institute Press, Annapolis, Maryland,2004) ISBN-13: 978-1591144410*

Honor, Courage, Commitment – Navy Boot Camp *(Naval Institute Press, Annapolis, Maryland, 2002); ISBN-13: 978-1591144380*

Further information about these books may be found at
www.navalwritersgroup.us

For More Information About The Pontifical College Josephinum:

Telephone: 614-885-5585
Email: Rector@pcj.edu
Visit us on the web at : www.pcj.edu